PRODUCTIVE CONFLICT

HOW TO **USE** TENSIONS, FRUSTRATIONS, AND DIFFICULT SITUATIONS **FOR GOOD**

Amanda **DUNN**

Solution Tree | Press
a division of Solution Tree

555 North Morton Street
Bloomington, IN 47404
800.733.6786 (toll free) / 812.336.7700
FAX: 812.336.7790

email: info@SolutionTree.com
SolutionTree.com

Visit **go.SolutionTree.com/leadership** to download the free reproducibles in this book.

Printed in the United States of America

FSC
www.fsc.org
MIX
Paper | Supporting responsible forestry
FSC® C008955

Library of Congress Cataloging-in-Publication Data

Names: Dunn, Amanda (Educator) author
Title: Productive conflict : how to use tensions, frustrations, and difficult situations for good / Amanda Dunn.
Description: Bloomington, IN : Solution Tree Press, [2026] | Includes bibliographical references and index.
Identifiers: LCCN 2026003611 (print) | LCCN 2026003612 (ebook) | ISBN 9798893741056 paperback | ISBN 9798893741063 ebook
Subjects: LCSH: School management and organization | Conflict management | School management teams
Classification: LCC LB2805 .D895 2026 (print) | LCC LB2805 (ebook)
LC record available at https://lccn.loc.gov/2026003611
LC ebook record available at https://lccn.loc.gov/2026003612

Solution Tree
Cameron L. Rains, CEO
Edmund M. Ackerman, President

Solution Tree Press
Publisher: Kendra Slayton
Associate Publisher: Todd Brakke
Acquisitions Director: Hilary Goff
Editorial Director: Laurel Hecker
Art Director: Rian Anderson
Managing Editor: Sarah Ludwig
Copy Chief: Jessi Finn
Senior Production Editor: Suzanne Kraszewski
Copy Editor: Mark Hain
Proofreader: Elijah Oates
Cover and Text Designer: Kelsey Hoover
Content Development Specialist: Amy Rubenstein
Associate Editor: Elijah Oates
Editorial Assistant: Madison Chartier

ACKNOWLEDGMENTS

First and foremost, all glory to God! I know this book would not exist without Him ordering my steps and clearing the path for the ideas to take shape. I would also like to thank my husband, Kyle, and daughters, Kara, Elizabeth, and Lauren, for your support and encouragement. Faith and family are my greatest sources of strength and joy.

I am so grateful for the Solution Tree Press Team. Thank you to Claudia Wheatley for believing in the concept and in me. Your nudges helped me to have confidence that we needed a book on conflict. Thank you, Amy Rubenstein, for your insight and guidance throughout the process. You are the Frank Lloyd Wright of content development! Suzanne Kraszewski, your eye for clarity is unmatched, and it was an honor to work with you.

To every educator with whom I have had the privilege to work, you are the reason for the research and the book. Thank you for sharing your peaks and valleys so that we could learn how to improve our school systems and change the trajectory of our students' lives.

Visit **go.SolutionTree.com/leadership** to download the free reproducibles in this book.

TABLE OF CONTENTS

Reproducibles are in italics

ABOUT THE AUTHOR XI

INTRODUCTION 1

How It All Began 2

Who Should Read This Book 3

The Goal of This Book 4

CHAPTER 1

Whose Job Is It? Clarifying Roles and Responsibilities in Your Organization 7

The Need for Clarity 8

Decision Mapping 10

Roles and Decision Making 16

Flow of Communication 23

Decision Fatigue 25

Scenario for Reflection: Roles and Responsibilities 28

Conclusion and Next Steps 29

Layers of Leadership 30

Chapter 1 Next Steps: Clarity 33

CHAPTER 2

What Is Happening? Common Conflict Categories in Schools 35

Curriculum Differences 36

Academics 36

Behavior 38
Instructional Design 40
Grading 41
Intervention 42
Extension 43
The Small Stuff 44
Personality Differences 45
Personality Traits 45
Work-Life Balance 48
External Pressures 49
Legislation and Standardized Testing 50
Community Partnerships and Parents 51
Social Media 52
Scenarios for Reflection: Conflict Categories 53
Scenario 1 53
Scenario 2 53
Scenario 3 54
Conclusion and Next Steps 54
What Is Happening? Common Conflicts 56
Chapter 2 Next Steps: Categorizing 58

CHAPTER 3

How Are We Responding? Common Approaches to Conflicts 61

Absorbing the Conflict 62
Positive Use of Absorbing 62
Negative Use of Absorbing 63
How to Decide When Absorbing Is the Right Move 64
Tackling the Conflict 66
Positive Use of Tackling 66
Negative Use of Tackling 68
How to Decide When Tackling Is the Right Move 69

Deferring the Conflict 70
Positive Use of Deferring 71
Negative Use of Deferring 72
How to Decide When Deferring Is the Right Move 73
Obstacles That Contribute to Choice 74
Scenarios for Reflection: Conflict Approaches 75
Scenario 1 75
Scenario 2 75
Scenario 3 76
Conclusion and Next Steps 76
How Are We Responding? Common Approaches to Common Conflicts 78
Chapter 3 Next Steps: Approaching Conflict 80

CHAPTER 4

What Are the Effects? Avoiding Conflict Spirals 83

Effects of Conflict on Task Completion 84
Effects of Conflict on Relationships 87
Effects of Conflict on the Organization 88
Go-To Orientations and Tendencies 91
Hot-Button Issues 94
Scenarios for Reflection: Avoiding Conflict Spirals 96
Scenario 1 96
Scenario 2 97
Scenario 3 97
Scenario 4 97
Conclusion and Next Steps 98
Task or Relationship Orientation? 101
Who are We? Using Personal Orientation to Avoid Conflict Spirals 103
Chapter 4 Next Steps: Avoiding Conflict Spirals 105

CHAPTER 5

How Can We Keep Conflict Productive? Improving Job Satisfaction and Motivation 107

Self-Determination Theory 108

Autonomy.. 110

Competence 112

Relatedness... 116

Ways to Improve the Three SDT Conditions 118

Structures 118

Responses... 119

Scenarios for Reflection: Improving Conditions 120

Scenario 1 120

Scenario 2 121

Scenario 3 121

Conclusion and Next Steps.................................... 123

How Can We Keep Conflict Productive? Creating Conditions to Improve Job Satisfaction and Motivation 124

Chapter 5 Next Steps: Improving Conditions and Motivation 127

CHAPTER 6

What Can We Be Proactive About? Implementing Structures for Success............................ 129

Mission, Vision, Values, and Goals............................ 130

Agendas 131

Norms 134

Meeting Structures.. 135

Resource Allocation 135

Scheduling 138

Leadership Teams.. 140

Training 141

Curriculum 141

Responses to Systemic Issues 142

Scenarios for Reflection: Structures for Success . . . 143
Scenario 1 . . . 143
Scenario 2 . . . 144
Conclusion and Next Steps . . . 144
Proactive Planning . . . 147
Chapter 6 Next Steps: Structures for Success . . . 150

CHAPTER 7

What Is the Plan? Creating a Comprehensive Conflict-Management Plan . . . 151

What to Do and When . . . 152
Summer . . . 152
In-Service Time . . . 159
First Semester . . . 161
Second Semester . . . 164
End of School Year . . . 165
Large-Group, Small-Group, or Individual Approach . . . 166
How to Develop a Training Plan . . . 167
Scenarios for Reflection: Creating a Comprehensive Conflict-Management Plan . . . 171
Scenario 1 . . . 171
Scenario 2 . . . 171
Conclusion and Next Steps . . . 172
Creating a Comprehensive Conflict-Management Plan . . . 173
Chapter 7 Next Steps: Creating a Comprehensive Conflict-Management Plan . . . 176

EPILOGUE . . . 177

REFERENCES AND RESOURCES . . . 181

INDEX . . . 189

ABOUT THE AUTHOR

Amanda Dunn, EdD, is an educator, coach, and presenter who specializes in Professional Learning Communities (PLCs) at Work® and response to intervention (RTI) system development and implementation. In addition to working with schools across the United States, she serves as a Sam Houston State University field supervisor for teaching candidates and previously served as an academic coordinator in the North Houston, Texas, area. She has over twenty years of experience teaching fine arts, special populations, and English, in addition to leading the PLC process and overseeing academic programs at the secondary level.

Throughout her career, Dr. Dunn has been named teacher of the year multiple times and in different teaching roles. She has earned degrees and certifications from Texas A&M University, LeTourneau University, and Sam Houston State University. She earned her doctorate in organizational leadership from Abilene Christian University. Dr. Dunn also earned a certificate in conflict management and is a trained mediator in the state of Texas.

Dr. Dunn is passionate about effective collaboration driven by efficient systems and conflict management that allow teachers, teacher leaders, and administrators to create environments and conditions conducive to high levels of learning and engagement for all students and adults.

To book Amanda Dunn for professional development, contact pd@SolutionTree.com.

INTRODUCTION

He always takes over! She never completes her work! How can anyone work with these people? Why can't we all get along?

How many times have you heard statements like these within your department, on your campus, or in your district? In conflict-filled organizations, professionals often spend valuable time trying to solve interpersonal issues instead of focusing on important work and results. Conflict is inevitable, but it doesn't have to be destructive. Conflict can be productive if it moves the organization forward.

Conflict researchers Joyce L. Hocker, Keith Berry, and William W. Wilmot (2022) define *conflict* as "an expressed struggle between at least two interdependent parties who perceive incompatible goals, scarce resources, and interference from others in achieving their goals" (p. 3). They further explain that conflict hinges on perception. This book focuses on the conflicts occurring in school systems, including those that come from external variables. The definition remains purposefully overarching and open-ended because conflict can occur in every corner of every team, department, campus, and district. Using conflict to move an organization forward is *productive*, whereas conflict is *destructive* when it causes work and relationships to break down.

Because conflict exists everywhere and with everyone, helping every member of the organization understand common conflicts, approaches, and the effects of our choices can keep campuses and districts moving forward. If we as educators want to create and sustain high-functioning departments, campuses, and districts, we need to recognize when conflicts are likely to arise and determine how to effectively manage them when they do. No one really wants to talk about conflict, but taking a proactive approach to conflict can make all the difference in improving schoolwide dynamics, increasing student learning, and accelerating teacher capacity building.

Countless studies and personal anecdotes point to the power of strong school systems improving learning outcomes for students (DuFour et al., 2024; Hattie, 2023; Javornik & Klemenčič Mirazchiyski, 2023). When individuals and groups struggle with destructive conflict, however, the learning organization can crumble. Destructive conflict cycles cause significant losses. Professionals leave their jobs because of conflict, or they are unable to do their jobs effectively because they are entrenched in conflict. Consequently, institutional knowledge is lost when there are no individuals in the pipeline prepared to move into open roles. Without a proactive approach and tools to address conflicts effectively, such losses will continue to erode the foundation of a school or district's culture, employees' job satisfaction, and their overall motivation.

The core purpose of the book is to guide you in developing a comprehensive conflict-management plan that decreases destructive conflict. The plan combines conflict-management skills with proactive structures to increase productive conflict. Although the concepts in isolation can help keep conflict productive, the full journey will provide a more thorough experience. Furthermore, an individual, team, or department can pick up the book and learn how to increase productive conflict. If you decide to use the book in a group, note that there will be opportunities for individual work and reflection, as well as for examining interpersonal relationships within teams and between departments.

How It All Began

As a new teacher leader, I wanted nothing more than to serve my team. I worked tirelessly to prepare lessons, materials, and data protocols, only to have team members become combative or frustrated. Knowing what I know now, I can see how my actions lessened their ability to respond to student needs and questioned their competence. In hindsight, I realize that I continued to do more, thinking I could create an environment conducive to successful collaboration, when what our team really needed was to participate in cycles of continuous inquiry and practice the art of teaching together.

I wish that, at the start of my career, I'd had a practical guide that gave me real-world strategies to plan for conflict and keep those conflicts productive. I think about every well-intended choice I made that caused more conflict. I consider every strained relationship I experienced that could have been improved. I reflect on all the times that going to work each day could have been less of a chore.

As I progressed into a campus leadership position, I considered the vast difference between the grace extended to students and that extended to other adults.

Some of the most empathetic teachers would eviscerate a peer during a team meeting. Furthermore, teachers and administrators who cared for others well, showing kindness even in overwhelmingly frustrating situations, did not show that same kindness to themselves. Why could we effectively diffuse conflicts between students and teachers but not between adults or internally? Working in a school system is taxing, but I knew we could find ways to continuously improve without losing our humanity.

This book results from years of study, both scholarly (Dunn, 2023) and on the job, that have helped me be more effective in managing conflict and advancing educational organizations. We can all get along, and I cannot wait to share with you the steps to accomplish that goal.

Who Should Read This Book

If you have experienced the negative effects of conflict within your organization, this book is for you! Truly, it is that simple. Everyone working in a school system benefits from learning about conflict management. This book is also for you if you work in an organization where everyone seems happy and completely compliant. If no one ever differs in opinions or challenges each other's thinking, the organization probably suffers from complacency and a lack of innovation through risk taking. No matter which group you fall into, conflict is inevitable for everyone at some point.

You might have picked up this book because you are in the middle of changing your school culture or have historically had a strong culture and now find yourself in the midst of destructive conflicts. You also may be in the process of turning around an underperforming school or trying to maintain strong current performance. No matter what situation applies to you, please note that everyone in the organization can benefit from this learning journey. When the entire staff—not just the administration—can manage conflicts more effectively, everyone can devote more time and energy to the work of student learning.

I firmly believe that very few people wake up looking for a fight, yet everyone experiences conflict. Learning conflict-management skills helps everyone, regardless of position, work toward effective resolution, which adds value to the organization. Reading this book and creating a comprehensive conflict-management plan (the focus of the final chapter) can lessen destructive conflict and increase productive conflict across schools and districts and from prekindergarten to grade 12.

The Goal of This Book

The goal of the book is not to get rid of all conflict; tensions and frustrations can move departments, campuses, and districts forward, improving learning outcomes for all students and increasing both job satisfaction and motivation for teachers (Shim, Finch, Cho, & Knapke, 2022). Rather, the goal is to increase the probability of conflicts remaining productive, resulting in organizational improvements and decreasing destructive conflicts where relationships are severed, people leave, or student learning suffers. We can use tensions, frustrations, and difficult situations for good when we have the tools and plans in place to keep conflict productive.

This book will equip you to identify and approach conflict in a productive way, but you will not walk away with a magic key or flowchart to eradicate conflict. That intentional choice avoids the dangers of an "if this happens, then do this" approach, which is not effective or desirable, since every conflict and the people within it are unique. School systems center on people, and every person deserves a personal approach when issues arise. This book will help you develop the knowledge and skills to increase the probability of keeping conflict productive.

Throughout this book, you will visit a fictitious school district, Productive Independent School District (ISD), to explore the various conflict-management skills and elements that help create a comprehensive conflict-management plan. Productive ISD has several campuses (all also fictitious), including ABC Elementary, Challenge Elementary, Discovery Middle School, and Platinum High School. These campuses and district provide realistic scenarios based on authentic experiences where conflict emerges among staff, who then build the conflict-management skills necessary to maintain productive conflict.

Each chapter focuses on a different component and various grade levels and departments. Although Productive ISD is not a real district, you will see your own experiences within it. Applying each scenario to your own context will provide opportunities for learning and help you build your conflict-management skills and plan. The following chapters provide you with the knowledge to do so.

- Chapter 1 helps you gain clarity about roles and responsibilities within your organization to reduce role ambiguity and improve communication. This chapter introduces the process of decision mapping, with chapters 2 through 6 providing more information for you to refine decision maps.

- Chapter 2 categorizes common conflicts to provide direction to specific areas of need. Knowing the categories and common areas of need is a pivotal step in selecting the most appropriate approach in future situations.
- Chapter 3 breaks down choosing the most appropriate approach to managing each unique conflict. You will analyze the positive and negative outcomes of each approach to better equip yourself to respond to conflict.
- Chapter 4 explains various activities and ways to learn about yourself and your coworkers to avoid conflict spirals. This chapter provides an opportunity for personal and group reflection for improving decision making when conflict occurs.
- Chapter 5 applies Self-Determination Theory (SDT) to educational contexts (Deci & Ryan, 1985). This chapter will help you and your organization improve employee job satisfaction and motivation.
- Chapter 6 explores structure implementation for proactively addressing potential conflicts. This chapter will help you identify structural strengths and weaknesses in preparation for the culminating chapter.
- Chapter 7 reviews key skills and concepts from the book so you can create a comprehensive conflict-management plan with a suggested timeline for the school year.

Whether you work through the book as an individual, team, campus, or district, you will discover the skills to bring clarity and consideration to the choices you make and conditions you create to keep conflict productive. Each chapter provides an opportunity to learn key elements, practice the learning through scenarios, think through next steps, and apply the learning to your context. Simply stated, *Productive Conflict* will help you take the everyday tensions you experience and use them productively to move your organization forward instead of spiraling into destruction. Working on conflict may not be easy, but it is worth it. You deserve to feel satisfied in your work, and students deserve to learn at high levels. When we learn how to effectively get along, we can accomplish both goals, so let's get started!

1

Whose Job Is It?

CLARIFYING ROLES AND RESPONSIBILITIES IN YOUR ORGANIZATION

School personnel work together every day to create learning environments for students. A multitude of people make thousands of decisions that increase or decrease the likelihood of students and adults thriving in the school and classroom environment. Many factors and nuances contribute to creating environments conducive to student success, and the potential for conflict is embedded in every facet.

In this chapter, we begin the process of creating a comprehensive conflict-management plan by unpacking the complex layers of educational organizations through the process of decision mapping. Benjamin Franklin described a process similar to decision mapping, which he referred to as *moral or prudential algebra*, in a letter from 1772. Some civil engineering practices include decision mapping, and it contributes to complex strategic decision making in multi-criteria decision analysis (Bouchart, Blackwood, & Jowitt, 2002; Comes, Hiete, Wijngaards, & Schultmann, 2011). These applications find value in exploring pros and cons to make the best choices or avoid pitfalls. For our purposes, a *decision map* is a tool to gain clarity, reduce ambiguity about roles, and define communication channels.

Here are a few questions this chapter explores.

- Who does what in your district, campus, department, or team?
- How do people in different roles interact with each other?
- Is there clarity about how information moves throughout the organization?

By the end of this chapter, you will have the tools to create a decision map for your district, campus, department, or team. Note, although the tools are in this chapter, you do not have to complete the full map before you move on to the next chapter. Decision maps are always evolving based on current needs and the people in each role. But do not shy away from working through this first step of gaining clarity and reducing role ambiguity because it will become critical to the process of understanding future conflicts and approaching those conflicts in your organization. After all, many times anger and frustration surface solely because people do not know what is expected of them or others.

Throughout this chapter and the rest of the book, you will find examples and scenarios involving conflict from the fictional school district Productive ISD and its various campuses. This chapter examines conflicts emerging from role confusion and responsibility frustration. Think about the times when you have thrown your hands up in the air and asked questions like the following.

- What am I expected to do?
- Who do I go to for help?
- How in the world can I complete all these tasks?
- Why do I have so many major tasks per week when my coworker has so few?

Missing the signs that someone is confused or overwhelmed happens all the time. Such conflicts can be productive when the initial tensions lead to organizational improvements. However, waiting for the tension to intensify into frustrated responses or, worse, for people to leave their positions, can destroy the organization.

The Need for Clarity

Like most school districts, Productive ISD has many layers of people, from the superintendent to principals, to teachers, to custodians, just to name a few. There is bound to be conflict when so many people are guiding the organization's day-to-day functions. Productive ISD teachers and administrators feel the daily strain of the pressure to improve student learning. The mounting stress placed on students, teachers, and administrators presents increased teacher burnout and turnover, staff and student chronic absenteeism, and inconsistent student growth scores.

But those issues are secondary to the increased conflicts at multiple levels within the district and at campuses. For Productive ISD, these are not cut-and-dry human resource issues with exact protocols to follow for reprimand or dismissal. Rather, the struggles lie in the day-to-day functioning of operating schools and ensuring students are learning.

Part of the frustration at Productive ISD is because of a lack of organizational research applied to schools. Unfortunately, many research studies focus solely on the principal or superintendent without considering those in the other layers. Some studies offer valuable applications for school principals (Jones & Thessin, 2015), but schools are not led solely by one person or an administrative team. Furthermore, a campus within a district often acts as its own organization within the larger organization, leaving a gap in understanding how each layer impacts others. Adding to the complexities, teachers and administrators receive training in all kinds of instructional practices and leadership strategies but never learn about how systems function. Even if educators want to learn more about this topic, they will be hard pressed to find best practices applied to schools. The high levels of training in education-specific topics lead to excellence in many areas, but if we do not understand how communication works or how to handle minor conflicts when information breaks down, we should not be surprised when people cannot get along. In starting the work of developing conflict-management strategies and adding conflict-resolution tools to our tool belts, we must first unpack the complex layers of the people who are pivotal to student success. As leaders strive to create environments conducive to teamwork, they must also balance the need for students to learn.

First and foremost, school leaders can no longer lead effectively in isolation. The rigors of modern education require systems of people working together to improve student outcomes. However, relying on complicated layers of people adds to the potential for conflicts. If we can increase the productive conflicts and decrease the destructive conflicts, the organization can move forward; however, this positive movement requires clarity about organizational roles and responsibilities. To achieve clarity, schools and districts must go beyond a typical organization chart, which depicts an organization's structure, or simple job descriptions to figure out *what* people are expected to do and *how* their specific skills contribute to common goals within the organization.

Without clarity, organizations are more likely to need formal leadership and hierarchies, which clog the flow of information. Additionally, increased formal leadership with one person controlling decisions can stifle creativity and innovation within the organization (De Clercq, Rahman, & Belausteguigoitia, 2017; Ziegert & Dust, 2021). For example, responding to student needs in a timely fashion becomes increasingly difficult if support roles are not clear or if a person feels they do not have the flexibility to solve problems with new solutions.

In the case of Productive ISD, staffing growth across the district in response to increased student enrollment has decreased clarity, specifically about decision making and communication. When the district was smaller, it was easy to stay on the same page within campuses and throughout the district. Some curriculum decisions were left to individual campuses or grade-level teams. Now, many curriculum decisions are centralized, placing greater responsibility on content directors. The additional decision-making job requirements also necessitate improving communication channels and unifying initiatives across campuses with different structures and needs. The process of decision mapping is the first step in addressing these issues.

Decision Mapping

Decision mapping takes the standard organization chart and turns it into a dynamic and flexible document that effectively and efficiently guides the flow of information throughout the organization. If your campus and district do not have an organization chart, start by creating a document that outlines who does what and who reports to whom. If you already have one, brush off the dust and determine whether the document is up to date and relevant to your organization's current structures and needs. Figure 1.1 shows Productive ISD's organization chart.

In figure 1.1, you might already start to see where problems could emerge. First, the job titles do not fully explain what roles entail. Second, the chart places people in silos when crossover between different departments and roles is constantly necessary. For example, a curriculum director does not intersect with a principal on the chart; principals are just an end point. Beyond the campus principals, there is no flow shown from district personnel to campus personnel. However, in reality, curriculum staff probably engage with teachers at campuses on a consistent basis. If the curriculum staff make a decision, they might share that decision with teachers during a professional development session. What happens if that decision does not match the campus principal's decisions?

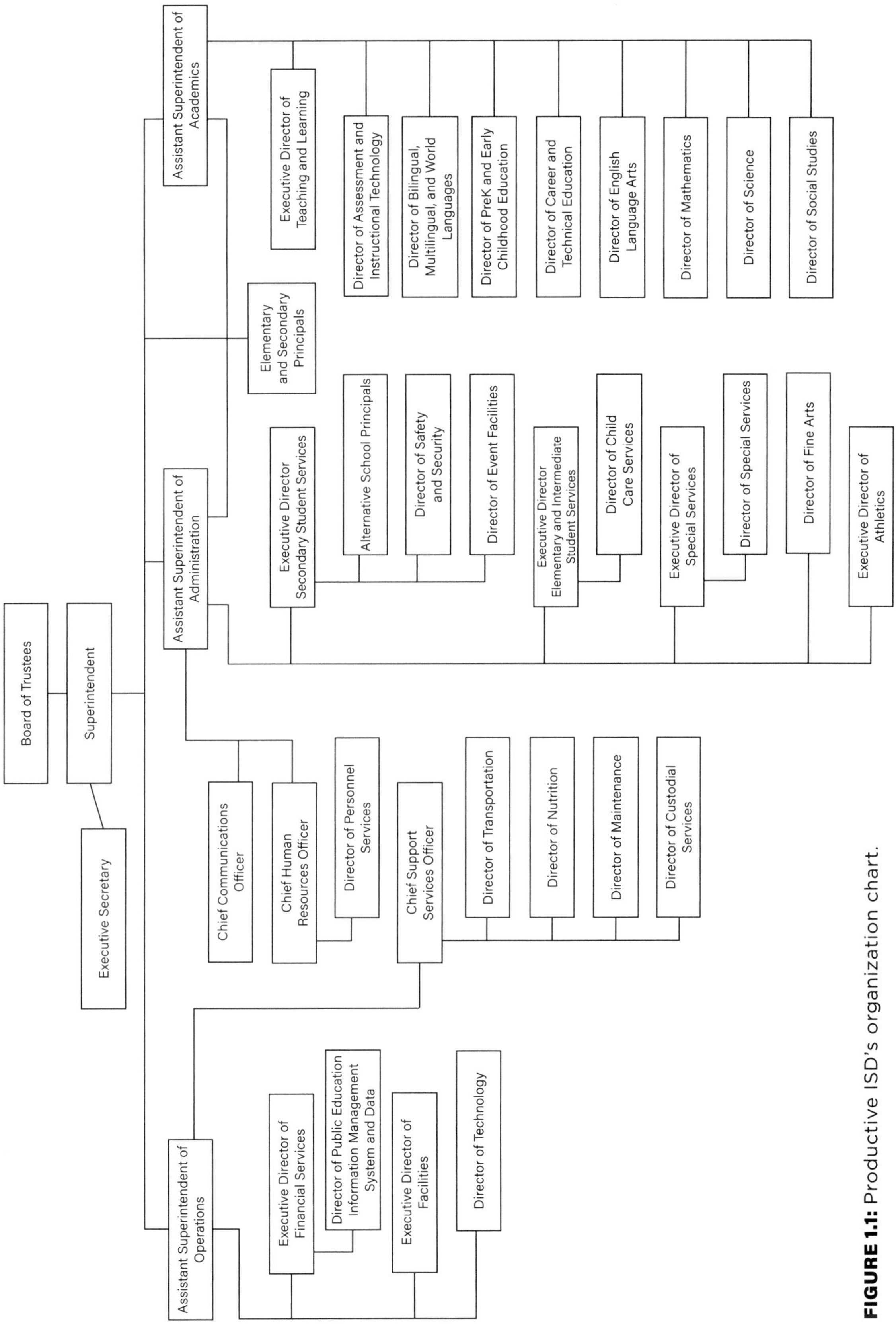

FIGURE 1.1: Productive ISD's organization chart.

Principals then create their own campus organization chart, meaning they oversee decision making and information flow at their campus. However, a district-level employee's job always involves teachers and students; thus, their reach goes beyond campus leaders—talk about overwhelming and conflict inducing. Consider how a principal structures the role to best use a campus instructional coach's strengths. Now, think about a district-level curriculum director trying to navigate one campus where the instructional coach only works with teachers and another where the coach also works with student groups. The principal leads the campus and makes those choices, but the curriculum director has communicated that instructional coaches work with teachers and interventionists work with student groups. The instructional coach is confused, the principal is frustrated, and the curriculum director thought protocols were the same as the campus where she taught ten years ago. So, how can we handle these crossovers of information?

A basic organization chart like figure 1.1 (page 11), with simple silos of people and positions, is a start; however, decision mapping uses more of a web structure than a flowchart, as figure 1.2 shows. While it looks messy on first glance, this chart allows leaders and educators to begin visualizing potential places where they need clarity and where there are crossovers. For example, the bilingual and multilingual learning (MLL) director takes the lead on students within the MLL program, but the assessment director takes the lead on testing the students; however, testing cannot occur without the technology department. The web structure also shows where one person is likely managing too many decisions. As you look at figure 1.2, pay attention to all the arrows pointing back at teachers. Teachers manage so many decisions each day that directly affect student learning. Without intentionally working through decision mapping, the risk of miscommunication increases, along with the potential for unnecessary or destructive conflicts.

Let's consider Genevieve, a teacher in Discovery Middle School who needs to order a resource to support their multilingual learners. Genevieve has no idea who to ask for the resource; she starts with one person only to be sent to another. Without clear roles and responsibilities and a decision map for the campus and district, the following are several possible options for who Genevieve might ask for the resource.

- The assistant principal who serves as the Language Proficiency Assessment Committee (LPAC) administrator
- The department chair who turns in order requests to the principal
- The curriculum coordinator for the subject area

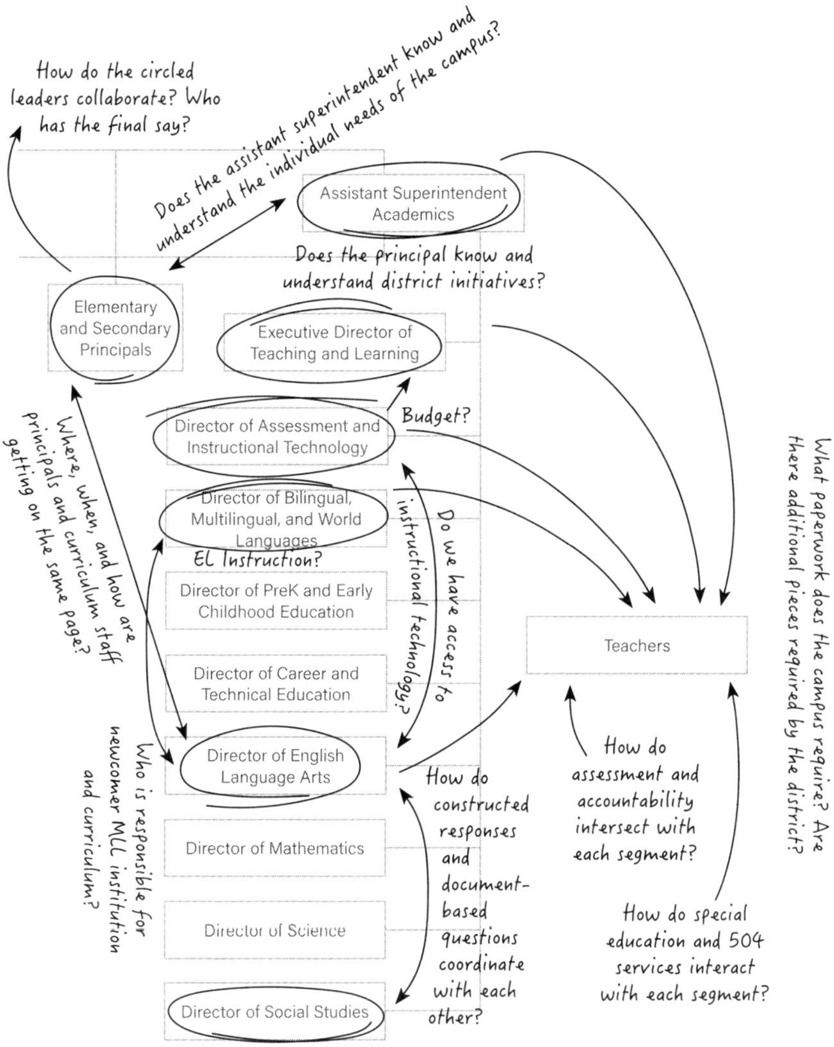

FIGURE 1.2: Web structure for Productive ISD's organization chart.

- The district director of MLL and bilingual services
- The Title III coordinator who might be at the campus level, district level, or both

Situations such as these often lead to frustration; Genevieve's request doesn't get approved in a timely manner, so she had to use her own money to purchase the resource. Teachers should be able to focus on student learning, not on who to ask for the necessary resources. In Productive ISD, there are people in the position of helping Genevieve get what she needs in an efficient manner.

To avoid confusion like this, schools and districts can create a decision map using the web structure. Productive ISD decides to start the process at the district level and then have principals create campus-level decision maps. Here are some basic steps at the district level. Note that the first four steps at the district level lead to steps 5 through 8 at the campus level.

1. District leaders create the organization chart like the one in figure 1.1 (page 11).
2. Each district department creates a web structure like the one in figure 1.2 (page 13). The web structure initiates conversation and awareness, adding dimension to the flat organization chart.
3. Each department defines its roles and responsibilities and compiles them in table form, as in table 1.1.
   - Role definitions should be clear and concise, providing direction for current and future employees.
   - Role definitions should stick to primary responsibilities with a brief one-sentence description.
4. District and campus leaders compare any overlap between departments. They start by determining how they will divide the areas of overlap between departments or where collaboration between different roles or departments will be necessary. Campus leaders then work on steps 5 through 8.
5. Campus administration creates a decision map based on campus administration protocols.
6. The principal uses the district- and campus-level materials to work with teachers and staff, comparing administrative connections to the district versus how the teachers connect to the district.
7. District and campus leaders compare their campus decision maps to examine similarities and differences to better communicate district information and streamline district systems. During this work, leaders honor and celebrate campus needs and differences. This will not be a one-size-fits-all decision map, as it must account for grade level, staff and student makeup, and other campus-to-campus differences.
8. Administration and staff revise the decision map throughout the year as needed, at least once per year.

Table 1.1 outlines some roles and campus connections to explore throughout the decision-mapping process.

TABLE 1.1: District Snapshot of Staff Connected With English Instruction

Role	Responsible for	Campus Connection
Assistant Superintendent of Curriculum	All district curriculum staff	All campuses
Elementary Director of English	• Literacy specialists • Interventionists • Elementary English teachers	All elementary campuses (grades preK–4)
Secondary Director of English	• Curriculum specialists • Advanced Placement, International Baccalaureate, and dual credit programs • Secondary English teachers	All secondary campuses (grades 5–12)
Director of Advanced Academics	• Gifted and talented specialists • Gifted and talented teachers	All campuses
Director of Instructional Technology	• Instructional technology specialists • Campus technology leads	All campuses
Director of Assessment	• Campus testing coordinators • State testing teachers	All campuses
Director of MLL and Bilingual Education	• Biliteracy specialist • MLL instructional coaches • Lead MLL teachers • Teachers of English learners	All campuses
Director of Special Education	• Special education instructional coaches • Co-teachers providing services in English classrooms • Behavior program specialists • Behavior program teachers	All campuses

Before we go any further into the mapping process at Productive ISD, know that decision-mapping work can be time consuming and overwhelming. This chapter explores the whole system to help you understand the process and where to begin. If you know it is not the right time of the year to complete the mapping process with everyone in your school, start with the groups, teams, or departments that seem to be struggling most with communication and conflict. The decision map can serve as a guide to quickly address problem areas plaguing grade-level or content-area teams, departments, or the campus or district.

The examples in the following section show the work Mr. Munson, Discovery Middle School's principal, did on the district English department segment of the district organization chart. Principal Munson established his own segment for his school and worked with teachers to create the final product for the campus in preparation for the district comparison meeting. During the district comparison meeting, the goal will be to unify the district and campus maps through dialogue. The campus portion will be pivotal to conducting a successful district meeting, as principals will be representing the needs of their campuses and helping to identify ways to improve clarity and reduce role ambiguity.

Roles and Decision Making

As Principal Munson starts to develop the English department segment of the campus map (see steps 5 and 6, page 14), he thinks about the English department's connections to district departments, beginning with curriculum. For Productive ISD, following the district curriculum map for the year is non-negotiable. Mobility among students is high statewide, making it crucial for teachers to stay on track with the standards and units the district has determined students must master. Principal Munson needs to dig into the department's responsibilities with the curriculum. He asks himself the following questions.

- What must campus leaders and grade-level or content-area teams adjust within the curriculum in response to student needs? For example, if a significant portion of student data shows a need for more time and support on a standard or target, can teachers determine the amount of time they spend on each standard within a unit?
- Are such decisions solely grade-level or content-area team decisions, or must these decisions be made collaboratively with another person in a different role?

The more Principal Munson digs into the process, the more crossovers he uncovers. He notes specific situations when teachers have been confused and frustrated. Many of those situations point back to the ambiguity they experience in decision making. This curricular decision mapping leads Principal Munson to consider assessment, special population services, services such as response to intervention (RTI), instructional support, and other district-staffed areas that add layers to the traditional organization chart. Figure 1.3 shows a portion of Principal Munson's rough draft.

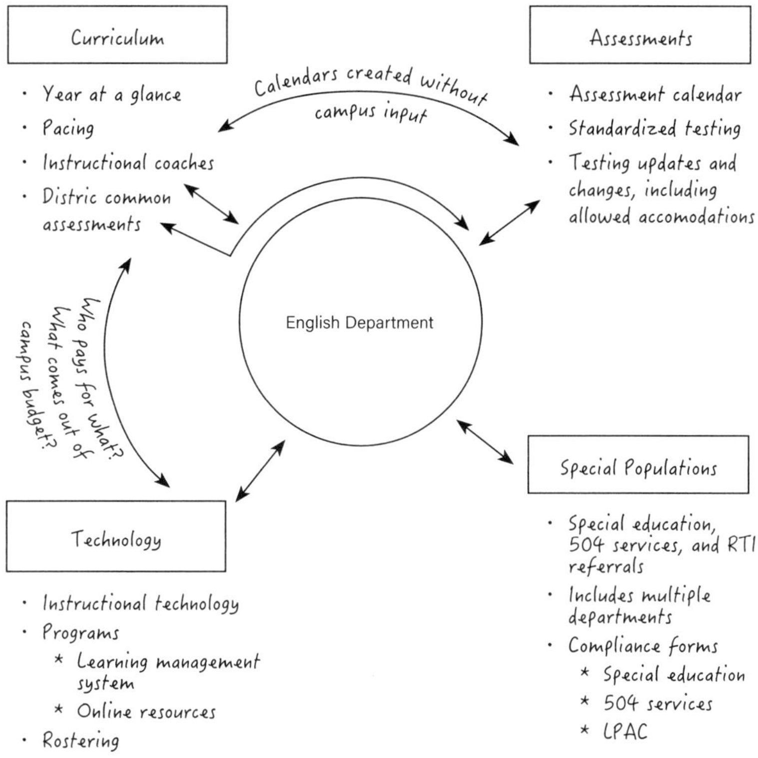

FIGURE 1.3: Principal Munson's rough draft of the English department segment of the campus decision map.

While mapping, it is imperative to visualize how information flows and crosses over. Look for places where the information flow becomes clogged. When spaces in the map are crowded with decision makers, chart out what is flexible versus what is non-negotiable to ensure that each person in the system has clearly defined expectations. Create the final product in collaboration with others. In this example, as Principal Munson worked on his rough draft, he tasked the English department chair, Yolanda, with completing a decision map from the teacher perspective. Figure 1.4 (page 18) shows a portion of what Yolanda created. As you look at the figure, notice the special populations section. Some compliance components will be non-negotiable. The mandated paperwork and due dates will not change. However, there is flexibility in the process for setting up meetings and communicating form submission requirements. A short conversation and a simple protocol could provide clarity to all involved with special education meetings and forms.

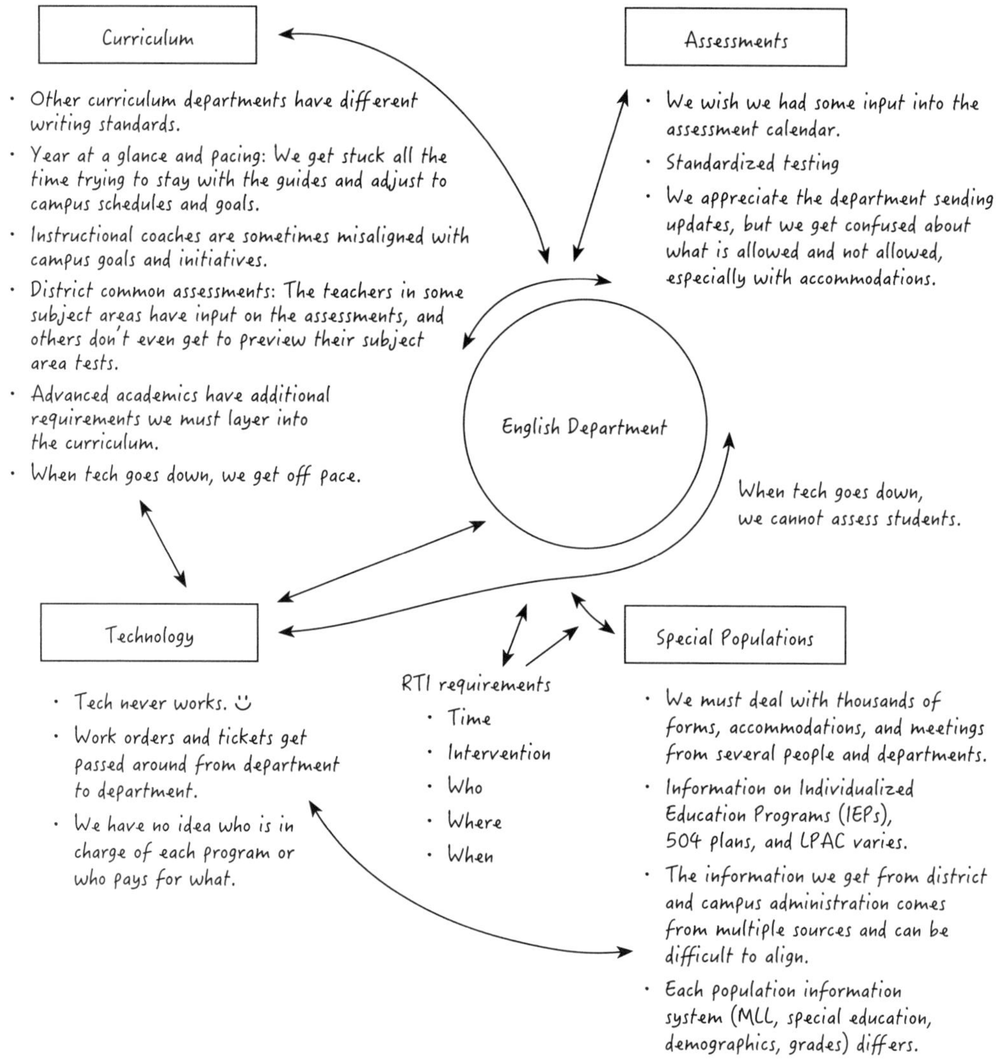

FIGURE 1.4: Yolanda's rough draft of the English department segment of the campus decision map.

When Principal Munson and Yolanda met to collaborate on the final map, there were several "Aha!" moments. Principal Munson thought he was aware of who did what and how messages were communicated to his staff. However, Principal Munson quickly began to see how teachers were constantly receiving information and directives from multiple sources with little consistency. He has encouraged teams to build backward from the assessment to ensure daily learning targets align with the evaluated standards. He knew some teams helped develop districtwide common assessments, but he was not aware that other teams did not see the test at all. He will address this inconsistency for clarity. There may be a reason for the difference, but Principal Munson cannot communicate what that might be without further information.

At the same time, it became clear that teachers had not considered certain legal requirements and the administrative aspects of finance that the principal and district-level staff must consider when making decisions. Yolanda wants to add a computer program to practice revising and editing. She feels strongly that the program departments have a positive impact on student learning and wants to expedite the purchase. Principal Munson let Yolanda know that computer programs must go through a specific purchasing protocol with the technology department. Based on that conversation, Yolanda revised the campus decision map. Figure 1.5 (page 20) shows the English department's final campus decision map.

The mapping exercise achieved the initial goal of surfacing the need for clarity and appreciation for why miscommunication can so easily turn into conflict. The maps, even after several rounds of revision, remain messy and difficult to absorb at a glance. This is expected and a purposeful part of the process. Working with the English department chair, Principal Munson determined where he could directly implement small but crucial changes to improve information flow and reduce staff frustration. Additionally, Principal Munson is prepared to take the maps to the district meeting and gather more ideas from others about how each department intersects with day-to-day campus functions (step 7, page 14).

To simplify the information in the maps, Principal Munson also creates a chart, shown in figure 1.6 (page 21). Once some of his questions are answered at the district meeting, Principal Munson will complete the mapping process with other departments.

Whew! That table contains a lot of information and questions. School staff make thousands of decisions each day, and starting with a web and then moving to a table will help organize observations, wonderings, and questions. Although the table contains a lot of information, Principal Munson cannot imagine how many blind spots were missed before beginning the decision-mapping process. Before, conflicts often seemed to stem from a lack of competency or even work ethic, but he can now see that many of them were related to a lack of understanding and clarity.

When working on your own decision maps, note that clearly defined expectations do not mean more work or paperwork. Reflect on your map and highlight the areas that have more non-negotiable expectations, especially fixed expectations that require paperwork. For example, special education and 504 services will be

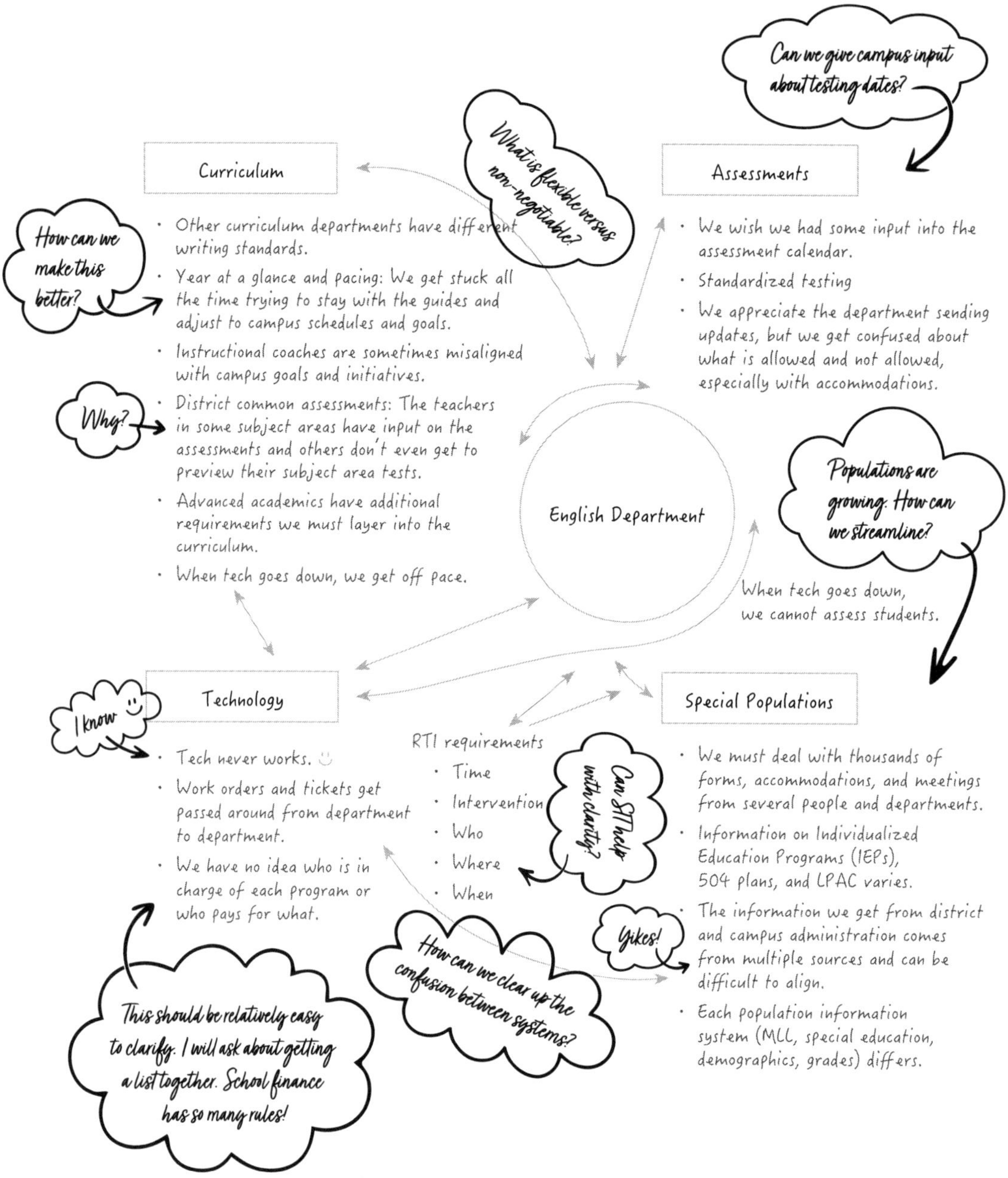

FIGURE 1.5: Segment of the final draft of the English department campus decision map showing the principal's notes.

Area	Roles Involved	Roles, Responsibilities, and Information Crossover	Questions to Inform Roles, Responsibilities, and Information Crossover
Curriculum	Curriculum directors, specialists, and instructional coaches	• Set year at a glance, unit sequencing, and pacing for each subject. • Create district common assessments. • Work with specialists and coaches to monitor and track student progress. • Crossover with other departments includes writing instruction, advanced academic requirements, tech needs, and assessment dates and expectations.	• What is flexible versus non-negotiable? • How can we figure out ways to stay on pace and account for student needs? • What input does the English department have on district common assessments?
	Campus leaders and administrators	• Work with grade-level teams to implement curriculum. • Address strengths and weaknesses for all teams based on data. • Alignment in messaging can differ between district and campus.	• How can we align messaging? • What are the "look-fors" during walkthroughs regarding curriculum implementation expectations? • Do our look-fors align with district requirements and messaging? • This seems like an area where crossover could be causing conflicts.
Assessment	Assessment director	• Create the assessment calendar. • Provide updates, including accommodation requirements.	• Can the campus provide input about testing dates?
	Special education, English learner, and advanced academics directors	• Collaborate on dates and procedures for all standardized testing for respective groups of students. • Campus staff can be overwhelmed with all the dates and expectations for the different groups.	• How can we use campus input and maintain organizational consistency throughout the district? • This seems like an area where crossover could be causing conflicts.
	Campus testing coordinators	• Implement testing requirements and train staff. • Provide more time for training and testing each year.	• How will we handle the additional workload across multiple roles as the number of required tests increases from year to year?
	Campus leaders and administrators	Coordinate testing logistics.	How can our systems better support students and staff?

FIGURE 1.6: Table form of the English department campus decision map.

continued →

Area	Roles Involved	Roles, Responsibilities, and Information Crossover	Questions to Inform Roles, Responsibilities, and Information Crossover
Special Population Services	Special education director	• Input forms, accommodations, and specially designed instruction. • Work with co-teachers and instructional-support teachers.	• Do we provide support to teachers (especially new teachers)? • How do we establish the working relationships between general education and special education staff? • Can we include administration in trainings to help with alignment?
	English learning director	• Determine instructional needs. • Handle LPAC forms and accommodations.	• Do we provide support for teachers? How? When? • Does some information cross over with special education? If so, can we streamline trainings? If not, can we align some of the forms?
	RTI director	• The student intervention team leads RTI. • Anyone on campus can submit students' names to the team. • The English department has a high level of responsibility in evaluating needs and providing interventions.	• Do we have additional staff to support intervention needs?

Technology	English department chair	• Oversee the following technology.
		  ¤ Learning management system
		  ¤ Various programs for special populations
		  ¤ Instructional technology
		  ¤ Online textbooks and resources
		• Specialized technology needs for assessment
			Who do we go to if we have difficulties with a program or need something added?

	Campus leaders and administrators	Facilitate technology needs and help troubleshoot.	What needs are communicated though the campus staff and what goes through the technology staff?

heavy on compliance with little room for flexibility in decision making and require paperwork as evidence. However, the instructional design for service implementation may be different from campus to campus or content area to content area. Teachers may need to track and monitor any differentiation, requiring more paperwork, or they may simply note it in the daily plans. During the mapping process, it is important to be clear about what your grade-level team, department, campus, and district requires. A lack of clarity leads to ambiguity, which can lead to more conflict. The key takeaway is the need for clarity and ways to visualize whether asking someone to complete the required tasks would be feasible. If tracking and monitoring are required, how much time will that work take? No one can add hours to the day, so time spent on other items must be adjusted. When you put pencil to paper, it helps picture how each piece fits together—or the chaos of expectations that can quickly create conflict.

Flow of Communication

The purpose of exploring the flow of decision making and communication through the organization is to improve clarity and lessen destructive conflict; however, the focus must still remain on student learning. As Productive ISD staff work through the decision-mapping process, they periodically revisit and reflect on the decision map to adjust and make improvements throughout the year (step 8, page 14) based on student results and to improve communication. Apply the following questions to your context while mapping (throughout all steps), being mindful of how your context contributes to the entire system.

- How do we communicate information throughout the organization?
- What do we communicate during a meeting versus through email?
- What is flexible and what is non-negotiable in communication?
- What is flexible and what is non-negotiable in decision making?
- Are the roles and responsibilities of various department and job roles clearly defined?

During the decision-mapping process, you will identify roles that make decisions for and communicate with a large number of people. Many times, this cannot be avoided. However, determining those spots, clarifying what is flexible versus non-negotiable, and removing ambiguity will still contribute to an improved probability of productive conflict. For example, the assessment coordinator will have to communicate with every campus, and many communication points will be non-negotiable directives attached to federal or state requirements. Why not be clear with everyone in the organization about which items are non-negotiable and which are flexible? Why not look for areas of flexibility to offset the rigid nature of the department? Additionally, there are opportunities to improve the flow of information and decisions in other areas. Ultimately, it is important to ensure that the number of decisions resting on a single role is manageable for timely responses and to avoid decision fatigue, which I discuss in the next section.

When people cannot get a timely answer, they are more likely to "go rogue" and decide for themselves or throw up their hands and say that no one is providing support. Some situations require problem solving, while others involve a direct protocol for everyone to follow. If members of the organization do not decide on these points and determine whether the information load is feasible, people will make mistakes or take too much time, which can affect morale. You have probably heard someone in your organization say, "Don't ask him; you will never get a response," or, "Don't ask her; she rarely gives out the right information."

In fact, communicating accurate and timely information has critical implications for the organization's development and productivity and correlates directly to employee engagement and retention (Gkiontsi & Karanika-Murray, 2016). Keep this in mind during decision mapping within your campus and district. Use these communication questions to evaluate the communication flow at the campus and district levels.

- What are our expectations for response times?
- How will we respond if the expectations are not met?
- How do we know the information is accurate, clear, and consistent?
- What will we do if information is inaccurate, unclear, or inconsistent?

Once you have completed an initial map and answered the communication questions, think about how you evaluate curriculum and apply the same process to communication, asking yourself, "Is what we are asking feasible and can everyone commit to our chosen expectations?" When organizations answer the communication questions, members of the organization do not have to wonder who to contact and how long it might take to receive an answer. We tend to blame others for miscommunication; however, when we consider that the system is a network of individuals, we can see miscommunication as a system failure (Gallois, Watson, & Giles, 2018). Everything we do in schools requires interdependence; we all have a piece of the responsibility. We can lower the risk of destructive conflict when each person within the system has a clear vision of their role and expectations for communication, thereby connecting individual actions to organizational goals (Gkiontsi & Karanika-Murray, 2016).

Decision Fatigue

In addition to clarifying roles and responsibilities, another reason to decision map and reduce clogs within the system is decision fatigue, an idea that developed from research on ego depletion (Baumeister & Vohs, 2007). The concept presents complexities related to self-regulation as a limited resource. If our ability to self-regulate becomes depleted through activity completion, we are less likely to control our responses effectively. Simply stated, *decision fatigue* describes the mental exhaustion experienced from making too many decisions in short periods of time. Our normal standards of functionality become reduced, leading to emotional reactions as well as inaccurate, unclear, and inconsistent choices, which feed into destructive conflict.

Let's look at how decision fatigue might affect Anthony, a seventh-grade English teacher at Discovery Middle School. Anthony arrives at school on time, prepared to assist any students who might need help with the essay they will be finishing in class. Before he can even unlock the door, three students show up for help with their thesis statements. Two of the students are in Anthony's classes, but one student has another teacher on his grade-level team. The two students from his classes, Elizabeth and Lauren, jumped right in and began working with Anthony on thesis writing, but Anthony could sense the third student, Kara, might be a little nervous about discussing writing with someone she does not interact with daily. Anthony only has twenty minutes of morning tutorial time, so he must choose how to respond to the students' needs quickly.

As Anthony begins to work with the students, more students enter with various needs. Jake needs to take a test, Tyler wants to borrow a classroom library book, and Gabrielle wants to jump in and work on thesis statements. Anthony bought a great new book that he wants to share with students, but he cannot give Tyler the new book because first he needs to figure out whose role it is to approve books and what that process entails. Anthony also has to text Jake's teacher so she can open the assessment within the testing site, and he must determine whether Elizabeth and Lauren need to hear the thesis information again or if they can work independently while he teaches Kara.

By the time Anthony gets to first period, his brain is swirling with all the things that happened during morning tutorials. Kevin, one of Anthony's first-period students, asks to go to the restroom immediately after the bell rings, even though all students know they cannot use the pass system during the first five minutes and the last five minutes of class. Before even considering whether Kevin has an emergency, Anthony says, "Just sit down, Kevin!" As soon as the words leave his mouth, Anthony regrets his emotional response and recognizes the impact on the rapport he's built with Kevin, who struggles to trust adults to be emotionally stable. How will this response impact Kevin and his future engagement in class? How will this interaction affect Kevin's learning and performance?

As you read the scenario, you may have felt deeply connected to Anthony's reality, or you might think he just needs better procedures and classroom management. No matter where your opinion falls, that does not change the fact that Anthony had to make many decisions with limited information before teaching his first class, and this is the norm on most days. Carrying this example throughout the day, Anthony must determine whether some of his students might be ready to write their essays with fewer sentence stems and other scaffolds. He will have to decide which students receive small-group assistance and which students require individual help. Some students will be absent the following day for a school-sponsored event, so Anthony must decide when they can finish the essay. By the time he goes to his English department meeting after school, Anthony feels absolutely exhausted from making thousands of decisions.

This is a normal day for most educators. Education scholars Sue Creagh, Greg Thompson, Nicole Mockler, Meghan Stacey, and Anna Hogan (2025) examine the increased workload and work intensification that contribute to teacher burnout, decrease well-being, and increase work-family conflicts. These scholars posit that school personnel not only do more within the workday, including nonteaching tasks, but they also work outside of school hours to complete accountability requirements. Creagh and colleagues (2025) define *work intensification* as "the rate of physical and/or mental input to work tasks performed during the working day" (p. 670). Every small decision staff members make within the day places more pressure on them. Those decisions add up throughout the day, creating daily chances for decision fatigue to affect each person's ability to effectively handle conflicts.

Whether in the classroom or in administration, staff face real and unavoidable decision fatigue. The decisions may not stop coming, but clarity can help us filter the decisions quickly and assess each situation more accurately before responding. Let's look at how the structures Discovery Middle School set up for its English department help lighten Anthony's load.

Yolanda, the English department chair, creates an agenda in advance for every meeting and always starts meetings with a review of norms and a few celebrations so the meeting remains productive. Anthony can quickly see on the agenda that there will be wrap-up time to offer Yolanda questions to take to an upcoming instructional leadership team meeting. This will be a perfect time for Anthony to ask about classroom libraries and the book approval process. He does not have to decide when it's appropriate to ask because the agenda guides the conversation.

Anthony also notes that the agenda includes a quick check-in to see how essay writing is going and adjust resource usage if needed. At that time, Anthony can check in to see if other teachers still see a need for sentence stems with English learners or if those students are ready to turn the prompt into a sentence on their own. One of the English department's team norms is to maintain a focus on all students during collaborative meetings. Therefore, after the meeting, Anthony will talk to Kara's teacher about her struggles with thesis writing. The agenda and norms are clear and concise, allowing Anthony to focus on the important tasks at hand instead of wasting valuable brain space on inconsequential decisions.

Imagine what types of conflicts would develop if the meeting expectations were unclear or the procedures for the meeting were inconsistent. Wasted time and lack of productivity would lead to tensions and frustrations within the team. Clear outcomes for meetings and standards to follow lower the number of decisions individual team members have to make. Anthony's example also highlights the value of decision mapping. Accurate, clear, and consistent communication creates a culture where people know what to do and who to consult when questions arise. When questions go unanswered (or get answered incorrectly), frustrations grow. We have already established a direct link between knowledge organizations, interdependence, and increased conflict. Unpacking the complex layers of the organization chart for clarity on expectations represents the first step in lowering the probability of destructive conflict.

Scenario for Reflection: Roles and Responsibilities

The following scenario highlights the importance of clarity in the organization. As you read, think about how decision mapping could improve the situation for Judy, a veteran second-grade teacher.

Judy feels confident, based on data, that students learn at a high level while in second grade and during their time at her school. Her second-grade team functions at a high level within the campus and district, but the start of each year brings about some uneasiness. Although Judy's district has strong processes in place, she still feels pressure to follow directives from various campus, curriculum, and operations leaders. Added to that, she must also process and implement revisions to state and federal laws. Last year, Judy waited for confirmation or information about time-sensitive questions, only to find out that her questions were meant to go to someone other than whom she had initially contacted. Because of this lack of clarity, time-sensitive decisions frustratingly had to be postponed. Judy thought it might be appropriate to make the decision with her grade-level team, but she did not want to overstep.

Reflect on the following questions in relation to the scenario.

1. What would be your first step to improve clarity in this situation?

____

____

____

____

____

____

2. In your current role, which parts of the problem could you control? Which parts would you have to ask for help with?

____

____

____

____

____

____

Conclusion and Next Steps

Decision mapping and analyzing how communication flows through an organization take time and honest reflection. Completing the initial process involves coordinating district leaders and campuses and revisiting the map at least once per year, or more often if needed. Although complex, decision mapping is worth the effort to avoid role confusion, decrease decision fatigue, lessen destructive conflict, and improve communication.

Before moving on to the next chapter on common conflict categories, use the reproducible "Layers of Leadership" (page 30) to identify the layers of leadership in your grade level, department, campus, and district and then answer the questions following the table. As you complete the table, continue to clarify and define roles and responsibilities. Use the "Chapter 1 Next Steps: Clarity" reproducible (page 33) to reflect on what you've learned about clarity.

Layers of Leadership

Individually or with team members or colleagues, identify the layers of leadership in your grade level, department, campus, and district, and then answer the questions below the table.

Area	Roles Involved	Responsibilities and Crossovers
Curriculum		
Assessment		
Special Education Services		
504 Services		
English Learner Services		

Area	Roles Involved	Responsibilities and Crossovers
Intervention Programs (such as RTI or Multitiered Systems of Supports [MTSS])		
Instructional Support		
Other		

1. What areas have the most layers of leadership in your organization? Are there opportunities for role clarity within those areas? What action steps would improve role clarity?

____

____

____

____

____

____

2. What areas might have layers that delay decision making? What action steps would improve timely responses?

3. What roles are listed in multiple areas that could lead to decision fatigue? Find one area where role clarity or responsibility delegation could lessen the number of decisions placed on one role. What action steps would provide clarity or transfer responsibility?

Chapter 1 Next Steps: Clarity

Individually or with team members or colleagues, use the following questions to reflect on what you've learned about clarifying roles and responsibilities.

1. How could we improve clarity about roles and responsibilities for staff?

2. What steps could we take to create a decision map?

3. What adjustments could we make to avoid communication clogs?

4. How could we ensure each person's communication load is both agreed on and doable in our decision map?

5. What are the best ways to ensure communication is accurate, clear, and consistent?

2

What Is Happening?

COMMON CONFLICT CATEGORIES IN SCHOOLS

In the previous chapter, you learned how to clarify roles and responsibilities, evaluate flexible versus non-negotiable decisions, and lessen conflict before it starts through improved communication channels. However, people still experience conflict even when an organization lays a strong decision-making and communication foundation. Recognizing the categories of conflict contributes to developing a comprehensive conflict-management plan by providing ways to group common conflicts. Identifying what is happening helps you select effective solutions to manage conflict.

When conflicts arise in schools, they typically fall into three common categories (Dunn, 2023).

1. Curriculum differences
2. Personality differences
3. External pressures

This chapter explores these three categories with examples and scenarios from another campus within Productive ISD: ABC Elementary. Remember, this chapter focuses on category identification, laying the groundwork for exploring conflict approaches in chapter 3.

At ABC Elementary, grade-level and content-area teams come together frequently to make data-informed decisions that impact student learning. Because teachers and administrators are in constant communication and rely on each other to serve all students well, there are many situations in which conflict can occur, either with open disagreement or internal struggle. Get ready to jump into the trenches because this chapter explores the various conflict categories campus and district employees encounter most often. By the end of this chapter, you will learn to categorize common conflicts, which will help you track issues that plague your campus and district the most and determine what areas might need proactive intervention. Knowing what is happening and where it is occurring, as well as the three common categories of conflict I explore in detail in the following sections, will be key components of your overall conflict-management plan.

Curriculum Differences

Although the negative effects of curriculum differences on learning outcomes are not widely researched, one study found that curriculum alignment positively affects learning outcomes (Alfauzan & Tarchouna, 2017). Scholars Abdullah A. H. Alfauzan and Nessima Tarchouna (2017) show links between student success and the alignment of learning outcomes with assigned tasks, which helps explain why tensions can emerge when school staff perceive curriculum differences. Curriculum differences can be rooted in misalignment and involve many issues related to student learning, including academics, behavior, instructional design, grading, intervention, extension, and the small details that can erupt into conflict. Conflicts in these areas can emerge between grade-level and content-area team members, campus administration, district administration, or a complex combination of several layers. In the following sections, you'll see examples of the kinds of conflict the staff of ABC Elementary experienced just one semester into the school year.

Academics

Imagine a world where we only need one perfect curriculum to ensure high levels of learning for all students. Did you laugh out loud or to yourself? Anyone involved in selecting new curricula can tell you that it is impossible to choose a perfect resource to use with students. It is also impossible to create a pacing calendar and curriculum guide that work perfectly for every classroom at every campus. To compound the issues, researchers struggle to reach consensus on the most effective ways to measure academic achievement and learning (Javornik & Klemenčič Mirazchiyski, 2023). Standardized tests, grades, and perception contend for the lead spot; however, one measurement does not tell the entire story of a student's learning. In other words, not only will what and how we teach be up for debate, but the best ways to measure learning will be contested as well. Therefore, conflicts over academic decisions are expected. The number of variables overwhelms decision making, but knowing how to categorize academic conflicts can help staff use the conflicts productively.

Student learning drives every process at ABC Elementary and in Productive ISD, which operate as Professional Learning Communities (PLCs) at Work (DuFour et al., 2024). Conversations and decisions about academics can lead to increased tension, even in PLCs with a focus on learning, collaboration, and a results orientation (DuFour et al., 2024). When categorizing conflicts as academic, the staff consider all the conflicts related to student learning. Table 2.1 breaks down several common academic questions and related tasks (DuFour et al., 2024) and potential conflicts.

TABLE 2.1: Academic Questions, Related Tasks, and Potential Conflicts

Academic Questions	Related Tasks	Potential Conflicts
What should students be learning in our classes?	• Determining essential standards • Identifying learning targets • Identifying proficiency measures • Creating unit plans • Reflecting on instructional strategies	• Personal bias toward particular standards, topics, or skills • Varied experience with the standards due to years of experience or consistency of standards • Conflicting opinions about the number of learning targets per standard
How will we assess student learning?	• Creating formative and summative assessments • Evaluating student data and work samples • Analyzing data	• Style of assessment • Assessment protocols • Levels of proficiency or mastery • Transparency during data analysis
How will we intervene when students do not learn the information we have taught?	• Creating and selecting intervention strategies • Determining structures and groups for implementation	• Types of interventions • Reassessment strategies • Ways to divide groups • Determining the difference between tiered intervention needs

continued →

Academic Questions	Related Tasks	Potential Conflicts
How will we extend and enrich student learning when students show immediate mastery?	• Creating and selecting extension strategies • Determining structures and groups for implementation	• Creating extension opportunities instead of assigning more work • Developing depth of knowledge without "stealing standards" from the next grade level

At ABC Elementary, the fourth-grade team meets weekly, using an agenda to guide their collaborative time. This week, the team plans to design a writing task and create the associated rubric. After taking the summative assessment independently, the team reviews notes and works to develop the writing task and rubric providing information on learning intervention and extension. The team quickly pulls the writing task together, but the rubric becomes a sticking point. One team member believes the point allocation should reflect the standardized testing rubric used to assess students at the end of the year. Another team member believes the rubric should focus more on student creativity and voice. The other team members can see the value of both ideas but struggle to determine how to marry the approaches.

In this scenario, the team is struggling with a curriculum conflict related specifically to academics. What typically happens in your organization when a similar situation occurs? For the fourth-grade team, the team leader feels the strain of guiding the team toward consensus but ultimately feels that she will have to choose a side, which will inevitably lead to more conflict and be detrimental to the team dynamics. However, she knows that avoiding the issue will create inconsistencies in what students are learning. The rubric focus will guide the design of the unit and initial instruction, so tackling the issue is necessary.

Behavior

Simple interruptions, from announcements over loudspeakers to behavior issues, can disrupt student learning through loss of learning time and breaks in concentration (Carrell, Hoekstra, & Kuka, 2016; Kraft & Monti-Nussbaum, 2021). Not only do these interruptions affect the moment, but they can also negatively affect focus for the rest of the class or block (Kraft & Monti-Nussbaum, 2021). Carrell and colleagues (2016) also note that student behavior, or even the behavior of peers, can have a detrimental effect on students' future earnings. While our focus does not include student-to-teacher behavior frustration, these ideas play an important role in adult tensions. Using instructional time to teach behavior skills and dispositions falls under the curriculum umbrella and can easily lead to destructive conflicts.

While the fourth-grade team experiences academic-related conflicts, the first-grade team struggles with curriculum conflicts related to behavior structures and the dispositions students should be learning and mastering. Applying the content of table 2.1 (page 37) to behaviors and dispositions shows that many of the related tasks and potential conflicts remain the same. Table 2.2 breaks down those behavior questions and potential conflicts.

TABLE 2.2: Behavior Questions, Related Tasks, and Potential Conflicts

Behavior Questions	Related Tasks	Potential Conflicts
What behavior skills and dispositions should students be learning in our class?	• Determining essential standards • Identifying learning targets • Identifying proficiency measures • Creating unit plans • Reflecting on instructional strategies	• Personal bias toward desired behaviors and dispositions • Varied experience with classroom management and opinions on the best way to manage a class • Conflicting opinions about the amount of time spent directly teaching behavior skills
How will we assess student learning?	• Creating objective measures of student behavior • Evaluating student data objectively • Analyzing data and determining ways to measure progress	• Style of assessment • Assessment protocols • Conflicting opinions about the amount of time spent assessing and measuring student behavior progress • Conflicting opinions about whether any instructional time should be spent on behavior instruction
How will we intervene when students do not learn the information we have taught?	• Creating and selecting intervention strategies • Determining structures and groups for implementation	• Types of interventions • Determining who should deliver behavior interventions • Determining whether and when to allot time for intervention
How will we extend and enrich student learning when students show immediate mastery?	• Creating and selecting extension strategies • Determining structures and groups for implementation	• Determining who should deliver behavior extensions • Determining whether and when to allot time for extension

For the first-grade team, behavior considerations apply to how individuals approach discipline and work behaviors in the classroom and hallways. Some teachers rely on structured environments with extensive procedures and rules, while others prefer a more relaxed environment with flexibility and minimal rules. The more structured teachers believe in explicitly teaching behaviors and dispositions, while the more relaxed teachers take an implied instructional approach. Neither strategy is inherently good or bad, but appreciating the differences and recognizing the effects on team decisions are critical.

Beyond personal preferences and styles, the campus and district do not have a specific behavior curriculum for all to follow. The team members are thankful for the autonomy because being required to use one particular behavior system can create conflict when that system contrasts with individual preferences. However, without behavior standards or a specific curriculum to teach behavior skills and dispositions, conflicts erupt over a lack of clarity about behavior expectations and ramifications of students not meeting those expectations.

Each time the first-grade team meets, behavior-related conflicts tend to monopolize their time. The teacher who believes in structure and rules wants to slow down the academic curriculum to explicitly teach work behaviors. She feels strongly that students need more than modeling and provides examples to support how not directly teaching work behaviors creates academic issues. Another teacher on the team feels the pressure of teaching foundational literacy skills and does not believe there is a single second to spare for teaching behavior skills. Because the team members trade students during intervention and extension time, multiple conflicts arise over student behaviors and student mastery of grade-level objectives. Although the first-grade team members have started working on the problem, they know that behavior and character curriculum decisions will involve other campus and district staff. The first-grade team leader makes a note to bring up the issue at the next campus leadership team meeting.

Instructional Design

After determining the knowledge, skills, and dispositions each grade level and course requires, instructional design work brings more potential for conflict. Many of these potential conflicts directly relate to each person's approach to teaching and learning. Even if everyone from the campus level to the district level agrees about what students are learning, those collaborative choices may implode when discussing how to present the information in the classroom.

When staff members consistently learn with each other and from each other, their focus on continuous improvement impacts the classroom for the better (Brodie, 2021; Stoll, Bolam, McMahon, Wallace, & Thomas, 2006). However, instructional design often centers on the personal craft moves teachers make to respond to student needs. Therefore, collective decisions about the unit's structure, pacing, and assessment dates create a constant tug of war. On one side, interdependence tugs toward consensus and a shared approach, which is in direct opposition to the other side, which tugs toward responsiveness and individuality.

For the third-grade team at ABC Elementary, this is the point where the strain tends to intensify because disagreement starts to feel personal. The third-grade team looks at standards and curriculum resources objectively, using end-of-year testing blueprints and the yearly outline for what to teach and the order in which to teach it. However, the team feels strongly that each essential standard needs three or four mathematics blocks for them to teach it effectively. The curriculum director holds firm that there is only time for one or two blocks, resulting in tensions flaring. The team members argue that they are best equipped to determine the pacing and activities that will maximize learning because they have based their decisions on data. The curriculum director does not disagree but must also figure out how to fit instruction for all the standards into the school year.

The team brings its concerns to the principal, but the principal remains stuck in the middle, trying to navigate the complexities of following district direction and responding to the needs of the teachers and students at his campus.

Grading

Grading ushers in more potential conflicts as teams, campuses, and districts hash out assessment questions. Assessing student learning and assigning a level of mastery branches off into decisions about everything from rubrics to what goes in the gradebook to grading guidelines. Whether you use standards-based grading, numerical grades, or a blend of approaches, consistency between classrooms helps alleviate potential pitfalls. Thomas R. Guskey (2024) states that many parents and teachers do not oppose grading reforms or changes to grading systems. The frustrations stem from the inconsistency, which creates a game to be played rather than a sustained focus on authentic student learning. Collaborating on the grading criteria and calibrating scores improves grading reliability (Brookhart et al., 2016) and helps maintain productive grading conflict.

Let's revisit the fourth-grade team struggling with creating a writing task and rubric. When the task created conflict, the team switched its focus to developing exemplars together. The goal of the switch was to figure out what the finished product should look like and work backward from there to determine the skill focus.

After each team member wrote an exemplar individually, it was easier for team members to see commonalities and collaborate using both perspectives. On one side, the teacher advocating for more creativity could recognize the need for explicitly teaching the form and organization. On the other side, the teacher advocating for following a process-driven structure could appreciate a need for exploring student creativity in word choice and sentence structure to avoid formulaic writing. In the end, the fourth-grade team used the initial conflict category to identify the problem and then used another conflict category to solve the problem. The team produced a rubric that represented the desired learning outcomes with associated point values to increase grading consistency between teachers.

Finding alignment from team members to campus leaders to district leaders can be challenging. In this situation, conflict occurs within the team, but the same conflict can occur between grade levels, content areas, and even schools. Every stakeholder brings a different perspective in determining the best examples of mastery. The combination of voices can improve student performance and grading consistency if the conflicts stay productive. Thus, as you categorize this type of conflict, consider the number of hands in the grading pot because each additional decision maker increases the conflict potential.

Intervention

Most schools have an MTSS or RTI system of intervention to address the needs of learners who do not meet current grade-level requirements for content mastery. These MTSS or RTI systems provide schools with a process to identify and intervene on students' behalf, offering a variety of leveled supports (Mattos et al., 2025; Navo & Williams, 2023). Even when teachers deliver excellent initial instruction, some students require extra time and support to learn academic or behavior standards. The response to students who need extra time and support then becomes paramount to student learning progress. Developing MTSS or RTI structures requires work from the whole staff. Here are just a few of the decisions that need to be made.

- Who provides Tier 2 and Tier 3 interventions?
- What time is embedded in the school day for Tier 2 and Tier 3 interventions?

- Who develops the lessons for Tier 2 and Tier 3 interventions?
- How can we ensure that students receiving Tier 2 and Tier 3 interventions are not missing initial Tier 1 instruction?

This list is not exhaustive, but each question presents potential conflicts. For example, the campus interventionist at ABC Elementary experiences scheduling constraints that require time flexibility for Tier 3 pullout programs. The time constraints require attention to avoid interfering with Tier 1 instruction, but the interventionist struggles to work with all grade levels and individual teachers to design a feasible schedule.

At the same time, the teachers are trying to balance responding to student needs for additional time and support with the need to keep a consistent schedule. One third-grade teacher has two students who leave for dyslexia services, two students who leave for speech services, and three students who leave for reading intervention. She also has one student who participates in both speech and dyslexia services. Three different staff members provide the services, and the teacher feels the strain of managing the schedules for her students. Adding to the frustration, several of the students participating in pullout programs struggle with the current standards being taught. She wants at least some of the dedicated blocks for Tier 2 and Tier 3 interventions to be devoted to current grade-level standards that students have not mastered or foundational skills that are keeping students from understanding grade-level material.

Immediately, the potential for constant friction becomes evident. The push and pull of who, what, when, where, and how swirl constantly when ensuring high levels of learning for all students. Also note, the frustrations are high, but they are not personal. The entire staff at ABC Elementary want students to learn at high levels and appreciate the expertise of the interventionists and various service providers. Staying focused on how to lessen frustration by improving the system keeps the staff from pointing fingers at the people involved. This situation shows why categorizing conflicts is critical to developing a comprehensive conflict management system. Any time we can improve a system rather than try to "fix" a person, maintaining productive conflict becomes more feasible.

Extension

While intervention tends to demand constant attention, extension conflicts are more likely to occur when trying to design effective extensions that go beyond extra work for students. For the kindergarten team at ABC Elementary, time and resource constraints add to the potential issues because increasing the depth of knowledge on a standard proves to be difficult work. Some kindergarten students come to school already reading, while other students do not know the alphabet. To address the varied levels of background learning, the team intervenes and extends often, but creating the extension pieces leads to conflict.

As the kindergarten team creates an extension, they realize the only time to implement it will be a thirty-minute block while interventions are also taking place, without any additional staff to help. The team only has fifteen minutes on their meeting agenda to figure out what the extension piece will be, and the team knows, based on the data, that they will need at least two different intervention groups to address two different learning misconceptions. With three groups needed—two intervention and one extension—the teachers will struggle to have enough staff to cover each group. One teacher wants to provide higher-leveled readers, one teacher wants to have the students work on a computer program that automatically adjusts to individual students' levels, and another teacher wants to start a project-based learning experience that could continue throughout the grading period. Their differing approaches result in a disagreement.

In my experience, one of three things occurs when facing an extension conflict.

1. The teachers each do what they are most comfortable with.
2. The teachers default to giving students who need extension extra work.
3. The teachers give students free time so they can focus on the students who require intervention.

Even when the teachers come to an agreement on how to extend the learning, they do not have the additional staff to facilitate the number of groups needed. Furthermore, if a teacher is a singleton who works at a campus where they are the only person teaching that grade level or course, they have the same problem of a lack of staff to support the extension work. As with the intervention issues in the previous section, conflicts with extension require systems improvement so the team can avoid being a breeding ground for conflict.

The Small Stuff

To close out curriculum differences, we will discuss the "small stuff"—all the little things that may seem insignificant but can erupt into major issues when there is conflict. If an issue involves part of the lesson, assessment, or monitoring process that will not affect student learning, then it is probably small stuff.

The assistant principal at ABC Elementary has noticed the small stuff concerns some teachers more than others. For example, the way student work is displayed in the hallway became a source of conflict for second-grade teachers. At first, the assistant principal was annoyed with such a trivial issue, but then she stopped to consider the cause of the conflict. One teacher used extra time at the end of a unit to incorporate critical thinking in an important standard. Another teacher used the time to have students add picture representations to their assignments. Neither teacher was wrong; both focused on responding to their students' needs. Additionally, research shows that both critical and creative thinking skills contribute to cognitive learning outcomes (Siburian, Corebima, Ibrohim, & Saptasari, 2019).

How does this relate to the hallway? The teacher who incorporated critical thinking did not want her students to see the other students' work hanging in the hall and feel that their work was not as exciting or complete. When this happened in the past, her students' performance improved because of the critical thinking applications, but some students were upset that they did not have time to add an artistic component. The other teacher feels her students performed at the expected level and needed to add the creative element to solidify their knowledge. The tension over the hallway display is small stuff, but it points to the underlying issue of time, which is not a small issue at all. The hallway conflict was also driven by personality differences between the teachers, which we explore next.

Personality Differences

There will be overlap when categorizing conflicts. For example, a curriculum conflict may be less about what is being taught and more about the personal preferences of the teachers. This is especially true of the small stuff. Although crossovers exist because every situation is unique and nuanced, personality differences fall mainly into two categories: personality traits and work-life balance.

Personality Traits

Personality traits contribute to conflicts through basic differences in personality, as well as differences in perceptions of conflict and preferences for handling conflict (Ayub, AlQurashi, Al-Yafi, & Jehn, 2017). According to researchers Nailah Ayub, Suzan M. AlQurashi, Wafa A. Al-Yafi, and Karen Jehn (2017), personality traits can be innate or learned, and having a variety of personalities is an expected and desired part of group dynamics and processes. Your teams, departments, campuses, and districts want people with diverse personality traits to come together and reflect the unique traits of the community (Pringle & Robinson, 2024). The goal of understanding conflict categories is to determine whether the root of the conflict lies in a personality trait or another category. Recognizing the difference in root cause directly affects the conflict management approaches we will explore in chapter 3.

It can be stressful to think about our personality traits and critique them. First and foremost, take a deep, affirming breath and recognize the one trait or attribute that most people like about working with you. For example, you could say, "People tend to like working with me because they can depend on me to get the job done." Now, take one more breath and own the fact that what makes you a desirable teammate can also make you the person who gets on everyone's nerves. This is the shadow side of your personality.

- **Positive personality trait:** Dependable, always gets the job done
- **Shadow side:** Takes over instead of letting others contribute to getting the job done

Now, take one more breath and recognize that the person with the difficult personality will be you at some point in the school year. Every single member of the organization will dig in their heels on an issue or be less than their best self when approaching a situation. When this happens, it is critical to remember that classifying a personality trait as solely good or bad creates a false dichotomy (Chappell, Cooper, & Trippe, 2019). Use figure 2.1 to quickly jot down some personality traits that make you great and then examine and note the shadow sides of those positive traits.

Positive Personality Trait	Shadow Side
People typically enjoy working with me because . . .	I tend to get on people's nerves when I . . .

FIGURE 2.1: Positive traits and shadow sides.

Visit ***go.SolutionTree.com/leadership*** *for a free reproducible version of this figure.*

Before the school year begins, make some time for staff to talk openly about their own positive personality traits and their shadow sides. Putting the strategy in action provides a chance for self-reflection and reframing. When you have a chance to own the strengths and weaknesses of the same trait, you are more likely to see how each side complements the other before leaning into the positive and resetting away from the negative based on the situation (Chappell et al., 2019). Additionally, the people you work closely with have an opportunity to reframe the frustrations. *Reframing* in conflict management simply means giving the conflict a new label, a new way to see the conflict (Hocker et al., 2022). In this context, reframing allows individuals to see the positive side of a trait in themselves and others. Here is a dialogue between the ABC Elementary principal, Mr. Liu, and the second-grade team leader, Jane, who tends to struggle with completing required grade-level tasks in a timely manner.

> ***Principal Liu:*** *Jane, this is the second time the district progress updates have not been completed for second grade. Is there something you need help with to ensure the reports are completed on time?*
>
> ***Jane:*** *No, I can do it. It is just that I am struggling to get the information from the other teachers. I don't want to push them too hard and mess with the team camaraderie that we have established.*
>
> ***Principal Liu:*** *Jane, we cannot miss this deadline again!*
>
> ***Jane:*** *Of course, of course. It will not happen again.* (Jane leaves the conversation defeated and on the verge of tears.)

Leaving the conversation, Principal Liu reminds himself of the tremendous job Jane does in creating an environment where the second-grade teachers trust each other enough to take risks. They are one of the most innovative teams in the building and tend to show significant progress in student growth from year to year. Although Jane sometimes struggles with holding the team accountable for certain paperwork-driven tasks, she uses her relationship-building talents to drive the team forward. After reframing how Jane positively affects the campus, Principal Liu thinks about how the conversation could have been different.

> ***Principal Liu:*** *Jane, this is the second time the district progress updates have not been completed for second grade. Is there something you need help with to ensure the reports are completed on time?*
>
> ***Jane:*** *No, I can do it. It is just that I am struggling to get the information from the other teachers. I don't want to push them too hard and mess with the team camaraderie that we have established.*

> ***Principal Liu:*** *Jane, you do an excellent job creating an environment where your team members trust each other enough to take risks and innovate. Student progress and learning would not be where they are today without your leadership. I don't want your team dynamics to suffer, but I do want to make sure we are adhering to district deadlines.*
>
> ***Jane:*** *Of course, of course. It will not happen again. I will set a repeating reminder and add it to the agenda in advance. That way, I will not feel like I am bugging them for the information. The time will be set, and the agenda will be focused on getting the task done on time together.* (Jane leaves the conversation knowing that she needs to balance her strong relationship-building skills with accountability.)

Jane's assessment of her positive traits and shadow sides might look like figure 2.2.

Positive Personality Trait	Shadow Side
• People typically enjoy working with me because I make them feel safe to explore new ideas. • People like my leadership style because they know their voices will be heard.	• I tend to get on people's nerves when I don't hold firm on deadlines because I don't want to hurt people's feelings. • I tend to get on people's nerves when I take too long to make a decision because I want everyone to share their thoughts.

FIGURE 2.2: Jane's positive traits and shadow sides.

One of the main reasons for breaking down the various types of conflict is to determine the best way to address individual instances of disagreement. With personality differences, it is personal! This makes issues more difficult to unpack. However, people are less likely to take personal issues personally if everyone sees how each personality offers both strengths and weaknesses. For example, when Principal Liu leads with the positive before prompting an adjustment, Jane is more likely to feel her contributions are valued but not above reproach.

Work-Life Balance

Another personality difference relates to each person's perspective on work and life balance. Research on work-life balance for educators reveals the increased challenges they face (Bisht, Uniyal, Johri, Qureshi, & Louati, 2025). Trying to strike a balance between the demands of the job and the demands at home can take a toll on everyone working in school systems. Staff may find unity in the struggle, but personality differences related to work-life balance may also contribute to conflicts.

Some people take grading or other administrative work home; others do not. (I am not suggesting any particular preference is right or wrong.) For example, one teacher prefers to stay after school for a few minutes to set up the room for the next day, while another might want to arrive a few minutes early the next day to do the same. The issues arise when a strain occurs between two or more individuals who become frustrated over the outside and inside balance.

The fifth-grade team at ABC Elementary decided to use the same slide decks for an upcoming unit that covers foundational standards for the remaining units. Team members want to teach, assess, intervene, and extend in the same way to ensure the entire grade level implements an agreed-on base level of mastery. They worked through how they want to present and assess the essential standards together. One of the fifth-grade teachers likes to think through the team sessions and then, after processing, work on the slides and materials in the evening. Another team member sticks to firm boundaries about not taking work home.

The next day, the slides are different because the teacher who prefers working in the evening has made some changes. The team agrees that the revisions improve the presentation and might clear up student misconceptions before a reteach is necessary. However, the team member who does not believe in working at home is seething. She knows the adjustments will benefit students and save them time throughout the unit, but she cannot admit it because she does not want to encourage extra work outside of school. The teacher who consistently works outside of school does not want to stop and gets frustrated at the implication that she should. She needs time to process and often feels she is not ready to add her best ideas in the group setting.

This conflict category presents complex challenges because there is no clear-cut answer or correct choice. People must be able work in ways that make sense for them. In later chapters, we will explore ways to honor those choices and differences without crippling teams. For now, simply recognize that personality differences can be difficult to navigate for this reason.

External Pressures

External pressures compound frustration because they extend beyond the organization's control. According to education scholar Daniela Martinek (2019), external pressures on teachers, including educational policies, public opinion, and parents' opinions, can lead to increased control strategies in class due to the impact on educators' psychological needs. Furthermore, although schools had been somewhat insulated from external pressures, changes in policy and legislation now force schools into cultural and political disputes (Diehl & Golann, 2023). Although conflict work in schools should mainly focus on the controllable issues, schools must also deal with how external pressures lead to conflicts within the workplace.

Rarely, if ever, would anyone in a district or at a campus be able to completely change or remove these pressures, but they will drive many of the decisions made at the district, campus, and school-team levels. External pressures will also bring about many of the conflicts that quickly become destructive because of the lack of control to improve the issues. Although the list of external pressures is long, this section covers the external pressures of legislation and standardized testing, community partnerships and parents, and social media.

Legislation and Standardized Testing

Consider the pressure of understanding legislation and the requirements of standardized testing. In the United States and Canada, most schools are judged each year on some type of standardized assessment. ABC Elementary shows significant achievement on the state assessment, but the growth measures for some student groups fall below expectations. All staff members feel the pressure of the exams, even though they do not have any control over the questions or the timing of the assessments.

For example, the fourth-grade mathematics team meetings run like a well-oiled machine. The team follows an agenda, beginning each meeting with team norms and a short celebration time. Team members work together well and have consistent evidence of learning for all students. When a new teacher joined the team, they quickly onboarded him and offered continuous support. Furthermore, they value the insight of the fresh voice to avoid blind spots in their procedures and protocols. The previous year, the team prepared for changes in the standardized testing for year-end student assessment. The team researched, exposed students to new question types, and monitored student progress throughout the year. Every data point led the team to believe the results on the standardized tests would match the results they had tracked throughout the year. However, that was not the case.

Although the team loss was less than the overall student loss across the state, it was enough to produce constant conflict for the first time among team members. The team members questioned each other on every decision, and the transparent culture they worked to create started to feel secretive. One teacher did not want to discuss data freely because she was embarrassed and fearful of getting in trouble with the administrators. The new teacher noted the amount of work and pressure placed on the students, but the department chair stated they had to push to improve standardized test scores. One of the administrators explained that she did not feel it would benefit teachers or students to make so many changes in one year, but the team wanted all students to learn at a high level. The external pressure crippled the team dynamics, and these conflicts can kill morale and confidence when left to fester (Youn, 2018).

Community Partnerships and Parents

Educators put a tremendous amount of work into developing strong partnerships with the community and parents. These strong partnerships can positively affect everything from student attendance to fundraising (Cummings & Olson, 2020; Sheldon, 2007). Even when relationships are mostly positive, they often can exert pressure on educators and school leaders.

Productive ISD's assistant superintendent of curriculum and instruction believes that the district has fundamentally improved student learning over the previous five years. The curriculum department remains focused on essential standards, quality assessment, and intervention and extension to achieve progress for all students. However, district staff also feel the community's pressure regarding drops in standardized test scores across several grade levels. Although the state as a whole demonstrates more significant drops, Productive ISD's community will view that variable as an excuse. The assistant superintendent's instinct is to weather the storm and continue with minimal changes, but she also recognizes the need for more oversight to ensure the school report card the community will see shows positive student results.

Optics can make or break schools and districts; how the community views the local school can be a source of support when there are minor setbacks or put a spotlight on slight declines. Perceptions can reflect reality and stem from a genuine need for improvement, or they can be rooted in false assumptions. Either way, these issues can seep into the organization and introduce conflict.

At ABC Elementary, a parent was unhappy with a perceived lack of support on a student discipline issue. The parent asked about the consequences for another student, but the school could not release that student's information. Because of this, the parent assumed the other student faced no consequences. The parent started to tell this story to other members of the community, and the teacher who wrote the initial referral was approached about the situation while grocery shopping. The external pressure created tension for several staff members who had not been involved in the original situation, and the conflict put teachers and administrators on edge to follow protocols exactly, especially when parents wanted private information. The parent then spread the message with a further reach by posting on social media.

Social Media

This conflict category would not be complete without a discussion of social media, a form of external pressure rife with potential for conflict. Social media is an integral part of daily life for most students, parents, and staff members. There are social media groups specifically dedicated to posting negative stories about schools. Students spend a lot of time on social media and might be participants or targets of mean-spirited content or attacks. The blurred lines between work and social media can further exaggerate the issues.

Consider what happened to the teacher who was approached by a parent while grocery shopping. After the negative interaction in the store, she was shaken, but that did not compare to the feeling of seeing what was being said on social media. The parent posted on the local "concerned parent" Facebook page about the situation. The parent used the teacher's name and other students' names. The parent perpetuated several falsehoods and the comments directly attacked staff members' character. The social media posts were reported to the district office, and the campus employees were able to show they followed protocols and legal requirements. However, they were not able to resolve the conflict or defend themselves on social media.

Some of the negativity can be kept outside of schools, but this is not the case when social media affects learning and results. In this example, the teachers, administrators, and district staff avoided interruptions to student learning. However, in other situations, social media has spread incorrect or incomplete messages, leading other parents to keep their students home from school. In one instance, Platinum High School had attendance below 60 percent for three days due to a social media threat. The external pressures directly affected student learning and progress, as many students missed days of instruction.

These conflict categories are meant to provide clarity about what conflicts you will most likely experience daily within your campus or district. Before we move on to common approaches to handling conflicts in the next chapter, take the time to reflect on which conflicts might be plaguing your grade-level or content-area team, campus, or district.

Remember—conflict can be positive! Locking arms, diving into this work together, and using challenging conversations to improve teaching and learning for *all* students and *all* adults remains the point. Do not get bogged down in all the ways these conflicts could spiral. The key is to reframe your thinking and consider how conflict can drive your organization out of ruts and through plateaus. The fourth-grade team at ABC Elementary, for example, worked through an initial problem—conflict over creating a task and rubric—and ended up in a better place for students by recognizing the type of conflict and working together to overcome it. That can be the norm at your school and district. Also, note that by the end of the book, you will be equipped with tools to handle conflicts effectively and keep them productive.

Scenarios for Reflection: Conflict Categories

The following scenarios will help you recognize common conflicts. As you read, reflect on similarities and differences from your experience.

Scenario 1

The first-grade team at ABC Elementary meets weekly and starts the year off strong with improved student results. However, the last few meetings have felt strained. When one team member wanted to share ideas on how to teach an upcoming skill, another team member said, "We don't have time to talk about that. We need to finalize our intervention plan for the upcoming assessment." This caused an issue among the team members, as one feels her voice is never heard and the other feels the team spends too much time on ideas without actually finishing the job.

Scenario 2

Recall the fourth-grade mathematics team from earlier in the chapter that is a model of excellent teamwork. In that example, the team came up with an instructional plan to prepare students for changes in the year-end standardized tests, believing their results would be as promising as those of other assessments throughout the year. Students did not do well on the new standardized tests, causing the team to plummet into constant conflict for the first time. Team members now feel the pressure of sticking to the essential standards while anticipating what the test will look like this year. Their last meeting ended with the new teacher and the department chair at odds over the number of practice problems and the increased homework load. The new teacher stated, "We are doing the right things. We cannot burn the kids out trying to anticipate what the state testing will look like. We need to stick to the standards and relax." The department chair responded, "Our jobs will be on the line if the community sees low scores posted in the newspaper for two years in a row."

Scenario 3

The assistant superintendent of curriculum and instruction recognizes that the current district initiatives have steadily improved student learning over the past five years. The curriculum department remains focused on essential standards, quality assessment, and intervention and extension to achieve progress for all students. However, they also feel the community's pressure regarding drops in standardized test scores across several grade levels. Although the entire state experienced more significant drops, the community will view that variable as an excuse. The assistant superintendent's instinct is to weather the storm and continue with minimal changes, but she also recognizes the need for more oversight to ensure the school report card shows positive student results.

Reflect on the questions in figure 2.3 for each scenario.

Conclusion and Next Steps

Being able to categorize conflicts leads to more opportunities for proactive intervention. The categorization process also provides a way for everyone in the organization to go beyond surface-level reactions or tensions to view root causes of conflicts. These skills will be pivotal to successful conflict management where productive conflict moves the organization forward and destructive conflict is minimized.

Before moving on to the next chapter on common approaches to handling these conflict categories, use the reproducible "What Is Happening? Common Conflicts" (page 56) to explore examples of conflict types on your campus or in your district, and then rank your examples based on frequency and the effects. Use the "Chapter 2 Next Steps: Categorizing" reproducible (page 58) to reflect on what you've learned about categorizing conflict.

Scenario	What conflict category does this represent?	What typically happens when this type of conflict emerges?	Are other decision makers involved in this type of conflict?	What can you control in this type of conflict?
Scenario 1				
Scenario 2				
Scenario 3				

FIGURE 2.3: Scenario reflection.

Visit ***go.SolutionTree.com/leadership*** *for a free reproducible version of this figure.*

What Is Happening? Common Conflicts

Individually or with team members or colleagues, explore examples of conflict types at your campus or in your district and then rank your examples based on frequency and the effects. When you are finished, answer the questions that follow the table.

Ranking Scale

1 = The most frequent conflict, and the conflict with the most negative effects

2 = Somewhat frequent conflict, and the conflict with many negative effects

3 = Infrequent conflict, and the conflict with some or few negative effects

Area	Examples	Ranking
Curriculum (Academic or Behavior)		
Personality		
External Pressures		

1. What common conflicts could you improve through more clarity or adjustments to the decision map?

____

____

____

____

____

____

2. Compare your results to those you work closely with. Then compare with a person or group in a different role. What areas are similar, and what areas are different? Why are some issues more prevalent in specific segments of the organization?

____

____

____

____

____

____

Chapter 2 Next Steps: Categorizing

Individually or with team members or colleagues, use the following questions to reflect on what you've learned about conflict categories.

1. How confident are we about categorizing the various conflicts common in schools? What could increase our confidence?

____

____

____

____

____

____

2. What common conflicts plague our context or job roles?

____

____

____

____

____

____

3. What conflict similarities and differences do we see with people in other roles?

____

____

____

____

____

____

4. What areas of improvement do we see in our decision map?

3

How Are We Responding?

COMMON APPROACHES TO CONFLICTS

In the previous chapter, you learned about three common conflict categories in school systems: curriculum differences, personality differences, and external pressures. While recognizing the type of conflict impeding progress is an essential step, the next step will guide you to successful conflict resolution. To get into the mindset of this chapter, think about times when you used the same strategy to solve a problem with two different results. I can think of multiple times when I decided to tackle a conflict and improved capacity and relationships. I can also remember times when someone tackled a conflict with me, and I greatly appreciated that someone was willing to work with me on improvements. Conversely, I can also think of times when I should have slowed down and let the situation breathe before digging in. I can distinctly remember a time when someone approached a conflict without considering their approach, which severely impacted our rapport and my self-confidence. If you can relate, you probably remember the destructive situations in vivid detail, which contributes to why this work is pivotal to everyone in the organization. While working through this chapter, think about how carefully considering your approach to handling a conflict increases the likelihood of selecting the appropriate approach for each unique situation.

First and foremost, we will never get this right with 100 percent accuracy. The humanity of our work involves countless variables that contribute to conflicts ending in either positive or destructive outcomes. However, this chapter contributes to your comprehensive conflict-management plan by adding tools to better recognize the potential positive and negative outcomes of each approach. This chapter adapts general conflict management approaches (Hocker et al., 2022; Jin, Singh, & Yun, 2019; Pruitt, 2001) and presents three key approaches to conflicts in school systems.

1. *Absorbing* conflict means letting time pass for emotions to subside.
2. *Tackling* conflict means having a difficult conversation.
3. *Deferring* conflict means bringing a neutral party into the conflict.

These approaches can push individuals, teams, and departments experiencing tension and frustration toward either positive or destructive conflict. Understanding the approaches, combined with recognizing the type of conflict from the previous chapter, can help staff members make the best decision for each unique conflict situation. This chapter examines the three approaches to common conflicts from both positive and negative perspectives, equipping school staff and leaders to decide which approach is best for a given conflict.

We continue our visit to Productive ISD, exploring the three approaches through situations within departments at Platinum High School. No matter what grade level or role you currently serve in, put yourself in these scenarios to consider how selecting the appropriate approach can lead to productive conflict. Also, use this opportunity to reflect on past situations where this knowledge could have saved you from destructive conflict.

Absorbing the Conflict

The first approach to common conflicts within schools and districts is to absorb the conflict. When absorbing the conflict, individuals intentionally wait to address the issue. This approach allows time for heightening emotions to lower and can be positive if it involves active listening. However, absorbing can be negative when people purposefully ignore issues they should address. Furthermore, absorbing can also take the form of toxic compliance or gossip, which fuel destructive conflict. We will explore toxic compliance and gossip in the next section, but for now, note that both point to negative by-products of absorbing the conflict instead of determining the root issue that needs to be addressed.

Positive Use of Absorbing

Absorbing can be positive when someone simply needs to vent frustrations without intervention. For example, the mathematics teachers at Platinum High School regularly vent their frustrations about pacing within a curriculum map to the mathematics instructional coach and campus administrator. The team understands the rigor. They know the intensity will be counterbalanced through the essential standards process. They see that district personnel are following mandates that are not within their control. Knowing this does not make it any easier when the teachers try to carve out time for students who require extra time and support to master a standard or when the flu runs rampant, wiping out entire classes over a two-week period.

Often, staff already have a plan in place to solve the issue; they are just feeling frustrated and need an active listener to hear them at a moment of peak emotion. Trying to tackle the conflict or bring someone else in to help at times like this is not only a waste of resources but also tends to lead to negative outcomes. A quick check-in the next day normally leads to a less emotional response as individuals have had a chance to pause and collect themselves, realizing that there are structures in place to address their issues effectively.

Negative Use of Absorbing

The same situation could lead to a negative outcome if a teacher is feeling constantly overwhelmed and reaching out for a lifeline. At that point, absorbing equates to avoiding the issue, which can lead to destructive conflict. Many of the mathematics teachers at Platinum High School have been teaching for five or more years, mostly in the same content area. However, the department has three teachers who are new in their roles: Mr. Gold taught the freshman mathematics course for almost a decade, but he is new to teaching an advanced junior-level class. Mrs. Silver taught algebra at the middle school level for five years, but she moved to teach algebra at the ninth-grade level this year. Ms. Bronze taught one year in another district and is not accustomed to the structures and norms at Platinum High School for helping students and teachers.

Because of their new positions, each of these teachers needs assistance beyond the weekly team meeting to feel confident and competent in understanding the curriculum expectations, monitoring student progress, and intervening when students are struggling. Mr. Gold understands school protocols and curriculum documents but needs help with understanding testing rigors in an advanced, upper-level course. Mrs. Silver understands the content and assessment expectations but needs help with understanding the school policies and procedures. She also needs assistance in adjusting from teaching an accelerated middle school class to a base-level high school class. Ms. Bronze understands the content and assessment expectations but needs help with understanding curriculum documents and both school and district policies and procedures.

Absorbing the conflict in these situations would be detrimental to student learning and the teachers' job satisfaction. These teachers need to be heard and to have their concerns addressed in a timely manner through support structures from the team, department, campus, or district. The level of support and providers will depend on the situation, but complete reliance on absorbing will lead to destructive conflicts that could cause a drop in student achievement or lead a teacher to leave.

How to Decide When Absorbing Is the Right Move

The main difference in the two situations is the issue's persistence over time. The first time that a conflict becomes known, an active listening approach might be the best choice. Responding too quickly without thinking about the true need can turn something small into a bigger deal, so relying on absorbing initially gives time and space for the conflict to dissipate or to gather more information. Conversely, if the same issue continues to resurface, the right choice is to go beyond active listening and look for root causes and possible remedies.

In the science department at Platinum High School, absorbing the conflict was destructive from the start. Platinum High School is constantly striving for commitment over compliance. The administrative team at Platinum High School works closely with teachers to share leadership roles and implement systems that help everyone in the building commit to common goals rather than just checking boxes to comply.

The movement to commitment has been a multifaceted process that takes time, but within the science department, there is an element of absorbing that really equates to toxic compliance. Organizations implement safeguards to prevent toxic workplaces that are unsafe and reduce employee engagement (Rasool, Wang, Tang, Saeed, & Iqbal, 2021). Those systems are important and have tremendous value for organizational health, helping prevent bullying, harassment, and other toxic behaviors (Rasool et al., 2021). However, individuals and groups that complete every task without a true commitment or internalization of the common goals can be just as detrimental to improvement and cause just as many conflicts. The biology team says *yes* to everything, never argues different points of view, and always submits every required piece of paperwork on time.

You may be thinking that this complete compliance is positive, but it has stripped the department of innovation, creativity, and continuous improvement. At weekly team meetings and monthly department meetings, the team constantly absorbs every uncomfortable emotion and avoids any conversations that might lead to a difficult discussion, giving the illusion that the team is happy and high functioning. However, student growth scores remain stagnant, classroom referrals continue to rise, and some teachers in the department have broken ranks to voice concerns. Ultimately, toxic compliance maintains the status quo and strives for an absence of emotion. Constantly avoiding expressing feelings or even silencing questions over time often leads to a larger issue than it needs to be, turning what could have been a productive conflict into a destructive one.

You have probably experienced this in some form—a teacher, team, or department that checks every box without authentically digging into the student learning process. Members never ask questions of substance or challenge themselves. This team or department doesn't blink when a new initiative is introduced; they simply change the box to check and move on. These apparently happy people, however, can take down everyone around them as they fall. Their negative absorption of the conflicts might result in significant student achievement losses, a member quitting without warning, or someone cracking and leaving a meeting screaming and slamming doors. It can be difficult to get people back on track and address conflict in an effective way when they have been absorbing for so long.

Another destructive way to absorb conflict is gossip. Rather than addressing issues at their source, people share or listen to information or complaints that may or may not be true, stoking conflict. For example, at Platinum High School, the English department works with a district instructional coach once a week. The coach helps entire teams and individual teachers. One of the teachers has shared her frustrations with the coach over feeling a lack of support from the administration, specifically the grade-level assistant principal. She feels overwhelmed with some of the behaviors in class and feels some students receive less severe consequences than others. She tells the instructional coach not to say anything because she does not want to start a conflict with her supervisor.

At an assistant principals' meeting the next week, the assistant principal shares with the instructional coach that she feels great about the growth of the English department. The instructional coach tells the assistant principal about the conversation and perceived lack of support but wants to make sure that the information he shared does not get back to the teacher. The instructional coach does not want to lose trust with his teachers, which leaves the assistant principal in a situation where absorbing is the only option and a negative one. Trust would be broken if the administrator tries to solve the problem, but trust has already been broken through gossiping instead of addressing the situation.

You might be thinking, "Why can't people simply have a conversation with each other instead of blindly complying or talking to others not involved in the situation?" Handling conflict effectively sounds easy in theory, especially when you are the third party. Take a moment to consider, however, how many times you have fallen victim to the same fate. Knowing when the absorbing approach might be the right move is a great first step. Next, we explore when it might be the right time to tackle the conflict.

Tackling the Conflict

Tackling the conflict means meeting the conflict head-on. A simple conversation, an action plan for improvement, or professional development could all be viable options for tackling a conflict. This approach might seem to be solely positive. Indeed, tackling the conflict with clarity in a way that maximizes competencies allows individuals to feel respected and heard, which builds trust (Jin et al., 2019; Kolleck, Schuster, Hartmann, & Gräsel, 2021). However, tackling the conflict can also have a negative side. Addressing issues to shut down discourse, for example, creates an environment where people feel unsafe to share, leading to a loss of trust and negative conflicts (Chiriac, Forsberg, Thornberg, 2024; Hocker et al., 2022).

Positive Use of Tackling

Tackling conflicts keeps them productive when trust is present and continuously built. For example, at the weekly English team meeting at Platinum High School, Sharon, a teacher on the team, did not complete a task on time. Others on the team felt frustrated, so Linda, the team leader, addressed the issue with Sharon one on one. When talking, Sharon revealed that she did not feel she could produce a quality product at her current skill level. Writing assessment questions, specifically creating the answer choices, seemed overwhelming and intimidating. Sharon felt better about avoiding the task than being vulnerable with the team. She needed help, but she experienced a paralyzing fear of showing weakness and knew that talking about her fears and insecurities during team meetings would only be viewed as an excuse.

Sharon also shared that she sensed how frustrating instructional technology was for the rest of the team. For her, working with data programs and creating assignments in the learning management system were both easy and enjoyable. Linda realized that Sharon could help the team significantly reduce the time members spent each week trying to figure out how to build the modules and collect data, as this was an area of weakness for them but a strength for Sharon.

By tackling the conflict, Linda found a way to plan for improvements in Sharon's weakness and maximize competencies in her area of strength. Linda's plan for Sharon includes the following.

- **Week 1:** Sharon will take more responsibility with the technology, including building the modules in the learning management system and sharing with the other teachers. Linda wants Sharon to focus on the content as she is building and take note of any points of confusion within the weekly lessons.
- **Week 2:** Sharon will write two questions as she builds the weekly module. At the end of the week, Linda and Sharon will meet to cover any concerns from week 1 and review how Sharon's question writing is going.
- **Week 3:** The team will review an upcoming assessment this week. The assessment is high quality, but the team made a note last year that it needed two or three more questions on a specific standard to better assess mastery and student need. Every team member will write one new question, review, and select the questions that best assess the standard. Linda makes it clear to Sharon that this will be a low-risk way to measure her growth in question writing.
- **Week 4:** During the week 3 exercise, Sharon did a great job with the question stem and correct answer. She will continue working with Linda on crafting the incorrect answers to help the team quickly recognize student misconceptions and need. Sharon feels confident enough to participate in question writing and her team has been so thankful for her help with building learning modules.

As a result of the plan, Sharon simultaneously adds value to the team and improves her skills. Had Linda decided not to tackle the conflict, the team would have lost trust in Sharon over a perceived lack of effort or laziness. Sharon's incomplete work pointed to an issue rooted in a lack of capacity. Addressing the conflict directly opened a pathway to making the conflict productive.

Notice that Linda addressed the conflict one on one with Sharon first. Directly addressing conflict in this way follows a specific pathway, as shown in the following numbered list, to maintain productivity and trust (English Standard Version Bible, 2001, Matthew 18:15–17; Hocker et al., 2022).

1. One person addresses a conflict with another individually.
2. Two or three people talk to the individual about the conflict.
3. A whole group, team, or department addresses the conflict with the individual.

Jumping to address the issue as a group too soon can lessen trust, eroding the foundation of collaboration (Ayoko, Härtel, & Callan, 2002). On the other hand, the progression ensures accountability and continuous improvements to avoid complacency.

Negative Use of Tackling

When people are too quick to tackle the conflict, especially from a position of power, it can lead to destructive conflict (Ayoko et al., 2002; Hocker et al., 2022). At Platinum High School, the fine arts team includes art, band, choir, dance, and theater teachers, with one of the band directors, Malcolm, serving as the department chair. The moment tensions emerge within the team, Malcolm is quick to tackle the issue. He sometimes addresses team members one on one, but other times, he discusses the conflict in front of the team. Additionally, Malcolm tends to shut down questions immediately, especially those that contrast with his personal opinions.

At the last meeting, the team discussed the auditorium calendar for the next year. In the district, the feeder schools use the high school auditorium for everything from shows to awards ceremonies, as does the community. The theater directors requested streamlining the reservation process because it has become overwhelming to manage; the directors constantly deal with angry people promised a date to use the auditorium only to find out there is already an event. The theater director wants to discuss two options that might help the team decide what would work best.

- Have all auditorium requests go through the theater department
- Have feeder school programs go through the high school program to pick dates, and then have the high school program submit a request before finalizing the date

Malcolm does not support either option. He wants to be able to pick dates and add them to the calendar without going through any steps. He feels strongly that Platinum High fine arts should have precedence over any other ceremonies, awards presentations, or outside performances not directly linked to a high school program. The other directors see his point and want to discuss what will work best for the department, but Malcolm shuts down the conversation. He states to the team that he can sense the tension and does not want conflict. He tells them that he will make a decision and share it with the team at the next meeting.

This is only one example of many in which Malcolm tackles a conflict too quickly, coming across as abrasive and domineering. Malcolm does have strengths: He is always clear about what is happening across multiple fine arts organizations and does a great job of pulling together a large team of teachers with diverse teaching assignments. However, no one on the team really feels safe showing vulnerability or sharing their thoughts. One department member has already requested to move to a different campus, and another department member agrees with everything in meetings but then does something different when running her program.

Part of Malcolm's issue is his tendency to tackle every problem immediately; another part is the position of power he holds. At Platinum High School, the department chair title is simply a service position that marks one person as the go-between for administrators and teachers. Even though Malcolm does not hold any rank over the rest of the department, his words and opinions tend to carry more weight with the team, pressuring others to submit, with one team member choosing to escape and another abandoning transparency and her integrity.

How to Decide When Tackling Is the Right Move

Establishing trust, building capacity, and creating safe spaces for risk taking are paramount in deciding when to tackle a conflict. Within the English team, the initial conflict and follow-up conversation led to increased trust and a plan to increase capacity. Linda created a safe place for Sharon to share her weaknesses instead of feeling as if she were in trouble. On the other hand, the theater directors took a risk and offered up potential solutions to a scheduling problem, only to be shut down. Would you be open to offering your thoughts and ideas if one person always made the decisions?

When deciding whether to tackle the conflict, remember that questions do not have to be viewed negatively. Shutting down questions, as Malcolm did, is a negative way to tackle conflicts. When Malcolm sensed tension, his first response was to stop the conversation. However, questions can encourage collaboration. The fine arts department wanted to collaborate and find a positive solution that worked for everyone. Tackling the tension too quickly robbed the team of being able to improve the situation.

Leaders should also consider how they handle questions and not think of them as negative. (Why is a subordinate questioning the new initiative or choices I have made?) Questions, even when asked at inopportune times, can point to areas that need clarifying or future frustrations that can lead to conflicts. Tackling the tough questions can be the right move to help everyone understand the reasoning behind a decision. Even if a leader decides not to tackle questions, it is wise to note what people are asking and saying—it could help avoid future conflicts. Fear of questions often points to insecurity about the ability to answer or to a lack of trust in the motives of the person asking the questions.

Note the cyclical nature of tackling and trust. Trust is paramount to working together, and tackling a conflict can be productive if grounded in trust or if resulting in increased trust. However, when tackling becomes the go-to without considering trust as part of the equation, the results can be destructive. Tackling strategies, including asking questions, creating action plans, or providing professional development, provides a way to accomplish multiple goals: resolving the conflict and improving capacity. At the same time, tackling too soon or too often can erode trust and provide sound bites for disgruntled members of the organization to share as gossip with others.

Deferring the Conflict

Deferring in this context refers to acknowledging that we need help to keep conflict productive; we defer to someone else, possibly with more expertise, when we have reached the limit of what we are able to do on our own. When we decide to defer the conflict, we either send it up the chain of command or bring in a neutral party to help mediate the conflict. Either strategy can defuse the conflict or add fuel to the fire, depending on the situation. Additionally, deferring the conflict tends to be the most-used approach when people lack training and experience in managing organizational conflict (Dunn, 2023; Hocker et al., 2022). Indeed, conflict tends to be less frightening when someone else deals with it.

Before we continue, please note that this section focuses on common, everyday conflicts. We are not focused on conflicts that must be handled by human resources, such as those that require immediate reprimand or removal. Putting students or staff in danger, cheating on a state standardized test, or using funds inappropriately automatically go straight up the chain of command without question. We focus here on minor conflicts that can have major implications on community and culture when not handled properly.

Positive Use of Deferring

Deferring the conflict up the hierarchy can be productive, specifically after making initial attempts to address the conflict at the team or department level. For example, many different teachers make up the foreign language department at Platinum High School, and the campus expects them to align their instruction horizontally within the same language levels. For example, all Spanish I teachers cover the same content and follow the district pacing guide. The department also works vertically to ensure a cohesive experience from level to level in the same language. At the beginning of the year and throughout the first semester, Nadia, the department chair, reviewed expectations with the department. However, department staff are still struggling with Sven, a team member who doesn't adhere to the set standards. Sven often shows up late and rarely has the required pacing calendar for the upcoming month, which is affecting team performance and task completion.

Nadia has conducted one-on-one and team conversations with Sven, but he has not changed his behavior. At this point, Nadia plans to have a discussion with the assistant principal who appraises the department. Normal procedures for improvement have not helped, so the team is hopeful that the assistant principal will be able to bring about positive change.

When Nadia meets with the assistant principal, she brings documentation to support the need for moving the issue up the ranks. She highlights that students participating in the language programs at Platinum High School leave with a high level of fluency and score well on advanced exams for college credit. She attributes the success to the alignment within the department and fears that without intervention from a third party, student learning and vertical alignment will suffer.

The assistant principal takes the information and meets with Sven. They have a discussion that serves as a warning before a formal write-up. From that point, Sven must adhere to the standards or risk formal consequences. Sven loves his job and excels at student engagement and relationship building, but he lacks the organizational skills to stay on top of the requirements. He seeks help from a colleague and makes efforts to improve, which allows the team to maintain their positive student learning outcomes.

Negative Use of Deferring

The same approach of deferring conflict can have a negative outcome if the team does not have strong procedures in place or does not directly address the issue first. If the assistant principal, who at Platinum High School is also the person who appraises Sven's performance, were the first person to address the situation, it could have broken trust between Sven and Nadia, resulting in a defensive response. In this alternate scenario, Sven might have responded by revealing a list of wrongdoings and inconsistencies with other team members.

Have you had this experience? You try to address a situation only to have the colleague, student, or parent reply with, "Well, did you see what he did yesterday?" or "Why am I in trouble when she was doing something worse?" The same occurs when deferring without warning.

When a third party steps in to help, negative conflicts can develop when that person must choose a side. This year at Platinum High School, the science standards changed for all grade levels. A conflict occurred within the science department about whether they would share learning targets with students before or after participating in an exploring phenomena experience or experiment. The discussion went round and round before the team decided to defer to the assistant superintendent in charge of curriculum and instruction.

At this point, the assistant superintendent was not mediating—they were picking sides, which only exacerbated the conflict. Instead of deferring, the curriculum staff could have created an opportunity for data collection by asking teachers to try one of the methods and report back on the results to determine whether presenting the learning target before or after the lesson has positive results for learning. The original approach of deferring to a third party created factions within the department, and the assistant superintendent's opinions had no basis in data. If the team had moved into a place of inquiry and collaboration, they could have kept the conflict productive but also increased teacher buy-in on the final decision.

When it comes to gossip, let's revisit the example about the English teacher and the instructional coach. The assistant principal absorbed the information and did not address it, maintaining trust with the instructional coach and between the teacher and instructional coach. This might have avoided conflict in the moment, but it allowed the conflict to continue. The coach eventually shared the information with the assistant principal, and the assistant principal then addressed the situation with the teacher, who then felt threatened that the conflict would impact the assistant principal's evaluation of the teacher's performance. Even if the assistant principal had not allowed a conflict to affect the teacher's evaluation, the power differential introduces doubt. What began as absorbing the conflict in a negative way ends up with someone outside the initial conversation addressing the conflict, with the conflict becoming destructive to relationships.

How to Decide When Deferring Is the Right Move

Much of the work we do throughout this book in designing a comprehensive conflict-management plan is about creating clarity, understanding the needs of others, and solving root issues masked by constant conflicts. We want to solve problems and move the organization forward, which is best accomplished by the people closest to the situations. As a result, much of the work hinges on equipping everyone in the organization with conflict management tools and strategies as opposed to pushing every conflict up the chain of command.

However, even the most gifted communicators and most admired colleagues cannot solve every conflict. There will be times when the continued back and forth can destroy relationships between colleagues. The decision to bring another person into the conflict should not be the go-to first response when there are other resources and tools to transform conflict into organizational and personal growth.

To aid in the decision to defer or not to defer, consider whether you have laid the groundwork for a third party to enter the situation. Blindsiding someone with anyone outside the situation will be a recipe for destructive conflict, including but not limited to destruction of relationships, trust, and group dynamics. Going back to absorbing or tackling before deferring gives conflict time to breathe and lowers the emotional response, establishing the foundation before going to someone outside the situation. It's also important to note that deferring often goes to someone in a position of power. Sometimes it goes to a colleague in the form of gossip, but many times the power differential adds layers of additional conflict potential. Think about how those differences in power, without any warning, can amplify the negative consequences.

Obstacles That Contribute to Choice

Each choice someone makes when dealing with conflict is the result of several contributing factors. Job and conflict management experience, role clarity, and training (or lack of) can all lead individuals to their choice (Dunn, 2023; Hocker et al., 2022). Both teachers and administrators can answer the questions in figure 3.1 to determine what obstacles might interfere with choosing the best approach.

- Level of job experience and conflict management experience
    - If I am new to my position and do not know what my job truly entails, how will I know how to approach conflicts effectively?
    - If I know my position but have never learned conflict-management strategies, how will I know how to approach conflicts effectively?
    - Am I willing to grow in these areas?
- Role clarity
    - Am I empowered to address a situation from my current position?
    - Looking back at my decision map, is there still role ambiguity? Hint: Look for places that are constantly riddled with conflict, as these are often areas where people still do not have role clarity.
- Training
    - How do my levels of experience or clarity affect how I approach a situation?
    - Do I need additional training to improve my conflict-management or job-role skills? If so, do I know who I can go to for help?
    - Does someone I work with or supervise need additional conflict-management or job-role training? If so, who could train the person?
    - How can I assess whether the training results in improved conflict-management or job-role skills?

FIGURE 3.1: Questions for improving your conflict approach.

Visit ***go.SolutionTree.com/leadership*** *for a free reproducible version of this figure.*

At this point in the book, you can categorize conflicts (chapter 2) and determine a conflict approach. It should be clear that every situation is unique with an unlimited combination of variables, so decisions about which approach to use for a conflict will not always be clear. Nor will the choices that worked beautifully in one situation be easy to replicate in every situation. Furthermore, sometimes we must experience the wrong choice to know what the right choice is. We are humans who work with other humans; therefore, our conflict-management skills will require constant growth and expansion.

Scenarios for Reflection: Conflict Approaches

The following scenarios will help you recognize and consider approaches to conflict. We will revisit these scenarios in chapter 5, where you can consider whether your choice of approaches should stay the same.

Scenario 1

The science instructional coach assists several teams across Productive ISD. He has a positive rapport with most of the collaborative teams and individual campus administration teams. One campus, however, seems focused on compliance instead of commitment. That team checks all the necessary boxes, but many of the decisions they make together do not authentically impact each classroom. The instructional coach wants the team to dive into the standards together and use data to respond to current student needs, but the team members fear conflict may occur if they hash it out. They are happy with the status quo and push back whenever the instructional coach guides them away from superficially addressing lesson planning instead of digging deeper.

Scenario 2

After looking at an upcoming unit assessment, the algebra team at Platinum High School decides they need to adjust the number of questions on each standard to match what they have deemed essential and plan to monitor throughout the unit. Each member of the four-person team agrees to write two questions for their assigned standard. The team includes two experienced teachers who have been on the algebra team for five years, one experienced teacher new to the team, and one first-year teacher who completed his student teaching with the team the previous year. At the next meeting, one person—one of the experienced teachers—does not have their questions ready. The team facilitator is shocked that an experienced teacher isn't prepared, but the new teacher has two questions ready. The lack of preparation from an experienced teacher concerns the team facilitator.

Scenario 3

Although the International Baccalaureate (IB) film studies teachers are singletons at each high school campus in Productive ISD, their students take a district common assessment two to three times per year. The IB coordinator for the district finds that these check-ins help guide the teachers' instructional strategies and improve success rates on the IB tests. During the last collaborative meeting, the teachers agreed on specific protocols for testing to ensure valid and reliable results. Unfortunately, although two teachers followed the protocol, two teachers did not. The IB coordinator typically tracks the results and can predict success rates based on the common assessments; however, the skewed results present a problem.

Reflect on the questions in figure 3.2 for each scenario.

Conclusion and Next Steps

At this point, we have reduced role ambiguity and improved communication flow throughout the organization (chapter 1), explored different categories of conflicts to better understand what conflicts we experience (chapter 2), and learned about the different approaches to conflicts (this chapter). In chapter 4, we will work through ways to avoid having conflicts spiral into destruction.

Before moving on to avoiding conflict spirals, use the reproducible "How Are We Responding? Common Approaches to Common Conflicts" (page 78) to explore approaches to conflicts in your team, department, campus, or district. For each approach, think of at least two examples of when you used or witnessed the approach and reflect on the results of the approach. Then answer the questions that follow the table. Use the "Chapter 3 Next Steps: Approaching Conflict" reproducible (page 80) to reflect on what you've learned about conflict approaches.

Scenario	Reflect on each approach (absorbing, tackling, and deferring) and what it would look like for each scenario.	What conflict approach would you choose? Why?	What do you anticipate will be the positive outcomes of your choice?	What do you anticipate will be the drawbacks of your choice?
Scenario 1				
Scenario 2				
Scenario 3				

FIGURE 3.2: Conflict approaches scenario reflection.

Visit ***go.SolutionTree.com/leadership*** *for a free reproducible version of this figure.*

How Are We Responding? Common Approaches to Common Conflicts

Individually or with team members or colleagues, use the following questions to reflect on what you've learned about approaches to common conflicts.

Approach	Examples	Results
Absorbing	1. 2.	
Tackling	1. 2.	
Deferring	1. 2.	

1. Which examples might have been more productive if a different conflict approach had been used? Why? How might the outcome have been different?

____

____

____

____

____

2. Compare your results to those you work closely with. Then compare with a person or group in a different role. Which aspects are similar, and which aspects are different? Did anyone view the same common conflicts and approaches in a different way?

Chapter 3 Next Steps: Approaching Conflict

Individually or with team members or colleagues, use the following questions to reflect on what you've learned about approaches to conflict.

1. What common conflict approaches do we recognize within our organization?

2. What are the positive and negative outcomes associated with each approach?

3. What different perspectives might we encounter on the same conflicts and approaches?

4. How can we equip individuals to address conflicts more effectively?

4

What Are the Effects?

AVOIDING CONFLICT SPIRALS

It will be no surprise to educators that conflict impacts task completion, relationships, and the overall function of organizations (Ayoko et al., 2002; Jin et al., 2019). When staff members do not like or trust each other, they do not typically want to work together. Conversely, when staff members do not complete their work, they struggle to build relationships with each other. This cyclical nature makes spiraling into destructive conflict an unfortunate possibility. However, staff members who are well equipped to handle day-to-day conflicts can minimize the effects of those conflicts on task completion, relationships, and overall function, and reduce the possibility of the gridlock of conflict spirals.

The term *conflict spiral* refers to a pattern of escalation in which responses become increasingly negative, intense, and retaliatory (American Psychological Association, n.d.; Hocker et al., 2022). Conflict spirals are difficult to break, but even more frightening are the behaviors that accompany them. Individuals who usually respond to tension or frustration in a reasonable way will resort to low blows and petty behavior (Hocker et al., 2022; Johnson & Indvik, 2001). Even if the actions remain low level, the perception of those caught in the spiral adds fuel to the fire. Further indicating the importance of reducing conflict spirals, team research points to spillover effects on others, especially when power structures are present (van Bunderen, Greer, & van Knippenberg, 2018). In other words, when people around us, even from other departments or teams, get stuck in a spiral, the destructive conflict can affect others. The hierarchy within school systems—think of the chain of command from a staff member to the superintendent—creates power structures that contribute to the danger of getting trapped in a conflict spiral. Even when you are not personally pulled into a conflict spiral, it can still negatively affect you.

Well, that was not a fun couple of paragraphs, right? The different components of conflict, especially destructive conflict, scare us, and rightfully so. Getting sucked into a conflict spiral happens quickly, and you are normally inside the spiral before you even realize it. Learning skills that help you move through conflicts in a positive way is difficult work, but avoiding a conflict spiral is a compelling reason for that work. A critical step in avoiding conflict spirals, and their adverse effects on the organization's function, involves first recognizing your own tendencies and default approaches toward conflict. Then, share your findings with coworkers to implement checks and balances honoring individual contributions to the group without creating imbalances.

This chapter serves as an activity guide for disrupting conflict spirals by applying research-based strategies to personnel in a low-risk progression. Some sections will highlight fictional scenarios, while others focus on self-evaluation or collaborative relationships, to respect the level of comfort in discussing personal subjects in workplace settings. From our work in previous chapters, we now have detailed maps and charts of roles and responsibilities (chapter 1), we know what conflicts are happening (chapter 2), and we know how conflicts are typically handled (chapter 3). In this chapter, we explore the effects of conflict on task completion and relationships and then determine our "hot buttons"—those personal traits and biases that trigger stronger emotional responses. Recognizing these hot buttons in others and ourselves will add another layer to the comprehensive conflict-management plan, helping to lower the negative effects of destructive conflict spirals.

Effects of Conflict on Task Completion

Conflict over task completion usually happens when tasks are not completed or the timing of completion is not optimal (Jin et al., 2019; van Greunen, Venter, & Sharp, 2021). Breaking the concept down further, task completion relates to the following three variables (Jin et al., 2019; van Bunderen et al., 2018).

1. The procedural approach: How are tasks being completed?
2. The delegation of action items: Who is doing what task?
3. Personnel delegation: How many people will be working on the task or tasks?

For example, Mr. Bridges, the principal at Challenge Elementary, encourages shared leadership within and between grade-level teams. He considers shared leadership pivotal to school improvement. His focus is on creating an environment where teachers are considered full partners in leading the campus (Printy & Marks, 2006). Part of the shared leadership culture at Challenge Elementary is a result of the tasks required in service of a population with high numbers of English learners and students who receive special education and 504 services. Principal Bridges knows it is impossible to monitor and track every task without leadership and ownership from teachers.

One of the required tasks focuses on assessing and intervening to ensure all students learn at high levels. Grade-level teams are required to give at least one common formative assessment (assessment *for* learning) during the unit, but teams can decide the protocols for the assessments and how they will disaggregate, discuss, and use the data to improve student learning results. Within each grade-level team, many potential curriculum, personality, and external issues can arise as teams figure out how to complete the assigned task. When those conflicts develop, they affect the team's ability to get the job done.

The core of the task conflicts at Challenge Elementary involves how to complete the task. Most staff members assume they share the same mission, vision, values, and goals related to the task, but lately, conflict occurs when team members cannot reach consensus or agree about how to go about getting the job done. Specifically, writing the required common formative assessment used mid-unit to check for progress plagues several grade-level teams.

The third-grade team consists of experienced teachers from Challenge Elementary and other schools in the district, plus one new teacher. One team member wants to use the textbook quiz as a formative assessment, one teacher wants to write questions (splitting up the work), and one teacher, Adela, does not understand why they should have to use the same assessment at all. Let's break down the task and conflict.

- **Required task:** Use a common formative assessment at least once during the unit and figure out how to use the data to improve student outcomes.
- **Current conflict:** How will we complete the task? Who should be involved, and why is the task important to student learning?

Rafael, the grade-level team leader, knows they must complete the task, and he will have to answer to the principal. However, he has not been able to convince Adela why common formative assessments are important to helping students learn with a higher success rate (Andersson & Palm, 2018; Wiliam, 2018). Rafael has decided to take over writing the assessment and takes the lead on gathering data to make decisions about intervention and extension. He knows this takeover does not align with shared leadership and building a trusting relationship within the team, but he feels the pressure to complete the task before the next check-in with the principal.

As we have learned, when tasks are not completed, a job goes undone, or other people take over, it can lead to further conflict. If the job goes undone, student learning and results will be affected. Additionally, the trust in others to get the job done is damaged. When people step in and take over to accomplish the task, this quick fix can maintain student learning results for the short term, but resentment normally builds, destroying trust.

To avoid the negative effects of task completion issues, it is important to understand why the tasks are not being completed. The root cause could be something out of anyone's control, but it often points back to a capacity issue (Jin et al., 2019; Mauersberger, Hess, & Hoppe, 2020; van Greunen et al., 2021). People do really strange things when they feel unequipped to complete a task. A person who normally stays on top of tasks misses deadlines. A person who typically apologizes for missing a deadline acts aloof and unaffected. A person who usually manages their emotions effectively lashes out at others. If we can figure out the why, we can intervene and help. Rafael feels strongly that capacity insecurities may be the root cause of the issues with Adela, the teacher who does not want to give a common formative assessment. Adela's class includes students requiring specially designed instruction due to language barriers and struggles with specific learning disabilities. Rafael sees the detrimental effects of taking over the task and commits to a singular focus on individual student progress instead of overall passing rate percentages. He hopes the focus on progress will convince Adela and get a true picture of how much learning takes place within her classroom.

Rafael visits with Adela individually before the next team meeting and outlines the research behind giving common formative assessments while also celebrating her strengths in differentiation and scaffolding. He asks Adela to try the common formative assessment and intervention process once before completely giving up on the concept. He outlines the exact steps and previews the data protocol the team will use to inform their decisions. Adela agrees, and Rafael expresses appreciation for completing the required task.

At the meeting after the common formative assessment, Adela feels some anxiety because she knows her overall percentages fall below other teachers'. However, as she prepares her progress data, Adela realizes that most students showed improvements from the pretest, and she sees how she might be able to group students to improve student understanding before the unit test. At the meeting, other teachers look to Adela for help with struggling students. The task does not seem as daunting, and Adela can see how the task contributes to student learning.

The potential for task-related conflict increases in knowledge-intensive organizations (van Greunen et al., 2021), such as grade-level teams where sharing information and interdependence are high, but better training and improved capacity can lessen task-related conflict as role ambiguity decreases (Jin et al., 2019). Think back to how decision mapping contributed to task-related improvements. Knowing what is required and who needs to complete specific tasks helped Rafael as the team leader take responsibility for assuring the task of common formative assessment was completed. After Rafael initially made the mistake of absorbing the conflict, he tackled the conflict one on one with Adela and later with the team to get the task completed.

Task conflict can also affect relationships when conflict issues develop due to a lack of trust (Jin et al., 2019). The next section explores the effects of conflict on relationships. As you look at these different areas of conflict, continue to consider the cyclical nature of conflict and its overall effects on campus and district performance.

Effects of Conflict on Relationships

Relationship conflict often refers to how individuals experience arguments, tensions, personality differences, and emotions (van Greunen et al., 2021). Relationship conflicts can take root in perception or style as involved parties find a role within the workgroup or determine how their conflict approach relates to other group members (Hocker et al., 2022). Individuals might see or perceive a situation as conflict inducing. Perception is subjective; one person might see a situation as no big deal, while another is frustrated by the same situation. *Style* refers to how people approach group situations and handle conflicts with others. Both perception and style tend to be deeply personal, which adds to the level of care needed to keep conflict productive.

Most conflict research describes relationship conflict occurring because of task conflict, even though this reciprocal relationship is not fully understood (Jin et al., 2019). The idea that relationship conflict can lead to misaligned task completion is also valid, as team members might misjudge someone's suggestion based on an underlying relational issue (Jin et al., 2019). In simple terms, some issues emerge within relationships when people do not complete tasks. Conversely, some people do not have a positive relationship, which prevents them from completing the work.

Principal Bridges considers relationships paramount to student success at Challenge Elementary. The importance of student and teacher rapport remains a top priority, and Principal Bridges feels confident in his ability to help teachers cultivate positive relationships with students. However, he is struggling to help the adults foster the same positive attitude with each other. The first-grade team includes a high-performing teacher with a strong personality. Principal Bridges notices that any ideas this teacher puts forth are met with negativity by the team and shut down without discussion. At one point during a grade-level meeting, Principal Bridges thought two team members might be texting each other about the situation, and he definitely witnessed an eyeroll or two. How has he excelled at creating a culture of positive relationships between teachers and students while completely missing the signs of issues between teachers? Whatever the catalyst for the initial conflict, the relationship effects are more than visible now.

Effects of Conflict on the Organization

Although groups tend to be less trusting than individuals (Pruitt, 2001), improving team trust helps lessen relationship-related conflict (Jin et al., 2019). The problem is that relationship conflict breaks down trust. This takes us back to the cyclical nature of conflict within school systems. If we can build trust, the relationship conflict should lessen, which should also positively affect task completion. However, a breakdown in trust can destroy relationships and lower product output as well.

Whether task or relationship related, conflict will occur more frequently because school system members practice interdependence (Hocker et al., 2022; van Greunen et al., 2021), and both negatively affect the overall performance of the organization (Jin et al., 2019). Since Challenge Elementary focuses on shared leadership, there is potential for more conflicts to arise more frequently. However, task- and relationship-related conflicts can be used productively to move groups and organizations forward (De Clercq et al., 2017; van Greunen et al., 2021).

Hocker and colleagues (2022) note that the way individuals communicate with each other can create a conflict or reflect the current conflict. Think back to the example from the first-grade team. The eye rolling and the text messaging between team members could have started the conflict, or the actions might reflect the lack of relationship within the team. Additionally, communication between parties can produce a productive or destructive conflict (Ayoko et al., 2002). In the situation with the first-grade team, the conflict became destructive, and the probability of the conflict impacting student learning is high. Additionally, how the principal might initiate productive conflicts and manage destructive conflicts while avoiding complacency, all without decreasing innovation, is debated widely (Ayoko et al., 2002; De Clercq et al., 2017). It is difficult to determine what level of intervention would maintain an environment where people feel safe to innovate without becoming so comfortable that they are satisfied with the status quo in a negative way. However, research has found the following about conflict and its effects on organizations.

- Task-related conflict can benefit teams when individuals willingly share different ideas, facilitating innovation and problem solving (van Greunen et al., 2021).
- A learning orientation can allow teams to leverage task conflict into creativity (De Clercq et al., 2017).
- Even when the conflict seems to be moving into a destructive path, effective communication strategies move the conflict back toward productivity (Ayoko et al., 2002).
- Discussing differences focusing on the issue instead of the people involved helps redirect the frustration and infuse empathy into conflict management (Ayoko et al., 2002; Hocker et al., 2022).
- Effective communication strategies can also build necessary relational goals within the group. Relational goals determine how individuals interact in groups, how people want to be treated in groups, and how the group will be defined (Hocker et al., 2022).

Combining research and application, think about how each chapter covered so far contributes to avoiding a spiral into destructive conflict, which can have negative effects on task completion, relationships, and overall function of the organization.

- **Chapter 1:** Clarity lessens role ambiguity. When people know who does what, how different roles interact, and how to clearly communicate with each other, they are more likely to complete tasks and build trust. When organizations consist of people who get the job done and trust each other, they are more likely to function at a high level.
- **Chapter 2:** When tasks are not being completed or relationships are suffering, it is critical to identify the catalyst for the conflict. Knowing what category initiated the conflict can help individuals determine the appropriate approach for each unique situation.
- **Chapter 3:** Once we can isolate a possible conflict category, determining the appropriate approach can guide conflicts into a productive space. When we pick an approach that leads to a productive conflict pathway, the organization moves forward, positively affecting its overall function.

Not building a conflict-management plan and working on conflict-management skills can result in such destructive conflict behaviors as interrupting, avoiding, and arguing (Ayoko et al., 2002; Hocker et al., 2022; Johnson & Indvik, 2001). When destructive behaviors emerge, conflict management plays an essential role in salvaging an interaction and preventing the relationship from ending (Hocker et al., 2022). Furthermore, excessive criticism, defensiveness, withdrawal, and contempt can be signs of destructive habits that lead to conflict spirals. These conflict spirals can cause perceived threats and negative emotions to escalate the conflict (Hocker et al., 2022; Jin et al., 2019).

School systems operate with circular causality, suggesting that each person affects another, and patterns, rather than a distinct beginning point, exist (Hocker et al., 2022; Jin et al., 2019). In both the first- and third-grade teams at Challenge Elementary, if one team member had felt blamed for a problem, the potential to point to another as the actual cause would have started a conflict cycle. For example, imagine if Rafael, the third-grade team leader, had continued to absorb the conflict and the additional work to complete the required tasks. At some point, the conflict would have affected the team, and fault and blame would have started within the team.

Here are a few comments you might hear when conflict spirals are swirling.

- "He always takes over!"
- "She never completes her work!"
- "How can anyone work with these people?"
- "Why can't we all get along?"

At this point, any attempts to manage the conflict effectively will be complex and challenging because the conflict spiral moves further into a destructive space. The negativity usually causes conflict triangles to form in which one or more team members form a coalition (Ayoko et al., 2002; Hocker et al., 2022). This will bring back the gossip as factions form and align against a common target.

Go-To Orientations and Tendencies

Remember, we are not trying to eradicate conflict within school systems. In equal parts, we want sound systems and clear processes to anticipate with higher proficiency what might happen and how we might handle each unique situation. That sounds clinical and scientific, which is a necessary foundation, but the art is knowing the people working within the system. If we are not hyperaware of each person's strengths, weaknesses, and preferences, we will inadvertently start or stoke conflicts. To maximize each person's competencies, let's start with ourselves and our tendency to lean toward task completion or relationships within the workplace. To be clear, one is not better than the other. This is just to get a glimpse into your usual tendencies.

Once you understand your own tendencies, you can share the results with your team or campus. If your department or organization decides to share results, ask them to be mindful of the personal nature of this work. Trust will be paramount to successfully using the information to guide conflicts into a productive space. For example, I lean toward a task orientation. If I share this with my team and they proceed to call me "Captain To-Do" every time I walk into a room, more conflicts will be created than alleviated. Because of the personal nature and nuance, the activities will focus more on the individual work with potential applications to larger groups that you can adjust for use in your organization.

Use figure 4.1 to evaluate whether you have a task orientation or a relationship orientation. For each row, read the options in the second and third columns and circle which one is more representative of you. Avoid overthinking every situation—just quickly pick the one that you typically lean toward.

1.	I make the to-do list.	I make work fun.
2.	I keep us motivated.	I keep us on task.
3.	I make sure we concentrate on the work.	I make sure we explore everyone's ideas regarding the work.
4.	I make sure we get along.	I make sure we meet our timeline goals.
5.	I know the job requirements of each team member.	I know what each team member needs.

FIGURE 4.1: Do you have a task orientation or a relationship orientation?
*Visit **go.SolutionTree.com/leadership** for a free reproducible version of this figure.*

Now look at figures 4.2 and 4.3. Figure 4.2 shows the items that reflect a task orientation. Figure 4.3 shows the items that reflect a relationship orientation.

1.	I make the to-do list.	I make work fun.
2.	I keep us motivated.	I keep us on task.
3.	I make sure we concentrate on the work.	I make sure we explore everyone's ideas regarding the work.
4.	I make sure we get along.	I make sure we meet our timeline goals.
5.	I know the job requirements of each team member.	I know what each team member needs.

FIGURE 4.2: Task-orientation indicators.
*Visit **go.SolutionTree.com/leadership** for a free reproducible version of this figure.*

1.	I make the to-do list.	I make work fun.
2.	I keep us motivated.	I keep us on task.
3.	I make sure we concentrate on the work.	I make sure we explore everyone's ideas regarding the work.
4.	I make sure we get along.	I make sure we meet our timeline goals.
5.	I know the requirements of each team member.	I know what each team member needs.

FIGURE 4.3: Relationship-orientation indicators.

Visit ***go.SolutionTree.com/leadership*** *for a free reproducible version of this figure.*

Answer the following questions to reflect on your answers. You can discuss questions 2 and 3 with others you work closely with, or even larger groups, if possible. If not, consider the questions and your observations of others you work closely with.

1. Which orientation do you lean toward?
2. Is your team more task oriented or relationship oriented?
3. How do similarities and differences in task and relationship orientation affect your team, campus, or district?

This activity does not take long to complete but can be a worthwhile individual and team activity because it is a low-risk lead-in to productive conversation. Use the reproducible "Task or Relationship Orientation?" (page 101) with groups completing this activity.

Applying the research cited throughout the chapter, we recognize how conflict affects task completion and relationships on our campus and district, but we cannot implement, sustain, and maintain a high-functioning campus and district without the human side. When people can start with a short, low-risk activity to engage in a conversation about who they are and where they naturally gravitate *before* conflicts arise, it does not feel personal. Moreover, the best part is that task-leaning and relationship-leaning people both bring positive attributes to every sector of the organization. More work is actually required if most of the team leans one way, as an all-task orientation can lead to burnout and an all-relationship orientation can lead to complacency.

Hot-Button Issues

The next step in understanding what everyone brings to the table is unpacking the influence identity has on our perceptions and potential conflicts. In this context, identity centers on who we are, including our values, beliefs, and expectations (Horton, Bayerl, & Jacobs, 2014). We must figure this out as individuals, teams, departments, campuses, and districts.

Exploring identity helps us to do the following.

- Recognize identity threats
- Determine personal bias
- Figure out what matters most as individuals, teams, departments, campuses, and districts

For the purposes of exploring identity in school systems, we will look at our hot-button issues through a simple activity. There will be crossover between personal and professional hot buttons, but maintain primary focus on how your identity influences interactions with others in the workplace. We want to figure out who we are and how we move in the group to minimize destructive conflicts. Knowing our own hot buttons will help us recognize topics that elicit an emotional response so we are better equipped to stop and recognize the button before responding. Knowing others' hot buttons will help us be cognizant of topics that could lead into emotional and potentially destructive responses.

Here is a personal example to highlight the influence of identity on task and relationship conflicts. For me, education has been the great equalizer. Looking at my background on paper, I was statistically destined for failure at best and a life of crime at worst. However, I had teachers who stood in the gap and pushed me beyond my perceived potential. A big part of my identity is knowing where I came from and being immensely grateful for the opportunities to break the destructive cycles in my family.

So, how does this part of my identity manifest at work? I take every part of my job seriously. I know that every interaction with a student could help put them on a pathway to success. I can become easily frustrated with people who are flippant about the importance of education in students' lives. I also become highly agitated by terms like "those kids" because I *was* one of those kids. Hearing statements like "Those kids don't care" or "Those parents don't care" elicits an emotional response that I must process to avoid unnecessary conflict.

To combat my personal bias, one of my norms in every classroom or at every presentation I give is to assume positive intentions. That norm is for me as much as it is for the students or educators I stand before. Because of my identity, I can perceive a comment or discussion point as offensive and conflict inducing when that was not the person's intention at all. Everyone's experience is different, and they cannot know whether something might be hurtful unless I am transparent about who I am. By sharing portions of my identity in group settings, other people can recognize the need for sensitivity or why something insignificant to them might be a bigger deal to me. I am not advocating for starting out each year with everyone's life story, but we can explore some of what we bring to the table through a short activity about identity.

When completing the activity in figure 4.4 (page 96), working with a small group you interact with most is helpful. It is also helpful if you complete this activity as part of a team norm-creation process. To complete the exercise, list in the center circle the things that are most important to your identity in the workplace. Then, work your way to the outer rings to list things that are part of your identity but are not hot buttons. It is often helpful to start by thinking of the things that really bother you, the hot buttons that get pushed and send you into an emotional response. From there, work backward to determine the root, which is probably something important about your identity.

When sharing your circles, you are the gatekeeper of information. If you do not feel comfortable sharing, use that information for yourself to help in future conflicts. This can be a deeply personal exercise, so it will be important to respect everyone's chosen level of participation. If the small group feels comfortable sharing, the task and relationship activity in figure 4.1 (page 92) and the identity activity in figure 4.4 can help build trust.

These exercises also build connections between tasks, relationships, and overall function so members of the organization can recognize how their individual contributions and personalities contribute to the whole. These exercises provide a chance to deepen our understanding of each other's perspectives. At the risk of sounding casual about the importance of these strategies, it gives us a chance to "check ourselves before we wreck ourselves" or the groups we work closely with. Why does this matter? Because our students matter, and you matter! If the work does not get done, our students do not get what they need. If we do not trust our coworkers, we do not feel good about going to work each day. Both matter to the overall health of the organization and the probability of maintaining productive conflicts.

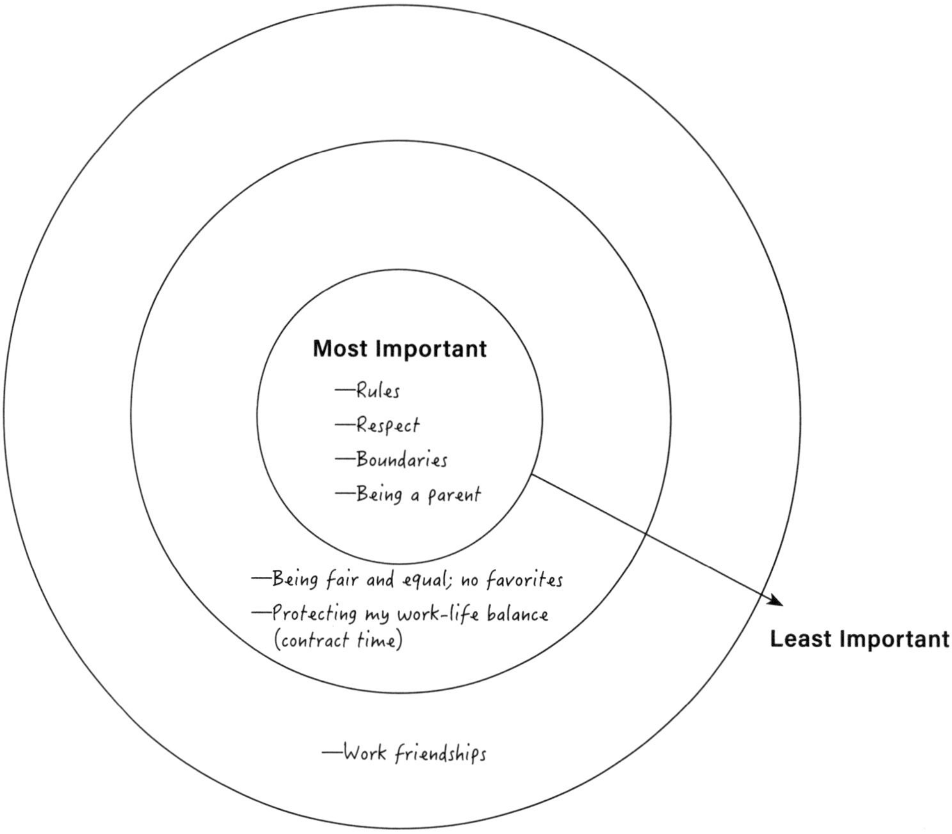

FIGURE 4.4: Exploring identity.

Visit ***go.SolutionTree.com/leadership*** *for a free reproducible version of this figure.*

Scenarios for Reflection: Avoiding Conflict Spirals

The following scenarios use recognizable, fictional characters that show the contrasting ideas of task versus relationship identity. See if you recognize the characters in your personal tendencies and identity.

Scenario 1

At its Wednesday collaborative team meeting, the fourth-grade team will decide on a plan for the upcoming unit. Each member has one specific task to prepare by the next Wednesday meeting. The agenda for the meeting is sent out on Thursday morning with outlined expectations (discussed and agreed on at the Wednesday meeting), giving team members ample time to clarify expectations and prepare. The team leader, Angela, begins the meeting with norms and a review of the agenda. A teacher, Meredith, promptly raises her hand to say she did not have time to complete her task. Dwight, another teacher, is furious. Angela is as well, but she is trying to stay calm and avoid confrontation. Other team members, Jim and Pam, are frustrated as well, but they have come to expect this behavior from the noncompliant teacher. Jim specifically just wants to keep the peace, get the job done, and go home to his family.

Scenario 2

The seventh-grade team discusses intervention and extension for the upcoming unit at its weekly meeting. As Hermione tries to review the team norms and agenda, one team member, Ron, tells jokes to the others, Harry and Neville. Hermione begins to reprimand Ron and the team about how she always has to do everything. Harry and Neville feel uncomfortable because they know how much work they need to do to prepare for the next unit. However, Hermione never lets them complete a task. To add to the stress of the moment, student performance on the essential standards in this upcoming unit has been among the lowest of the last few years, and the eighth-grade team has explicitly asked for the seventh-grade team to place more attention on this unit.

Scenario 3

At its weekly meeting, the eighth-grade team dissects data from the previous grade level. The student data points to some learning gaps on a few key standards. In the middle of the meeting, the team leader, Draco, addresses Bellatrix, the administrator who works closely with both the eighth-grade and seventh-grade teams to share his concerns. Draco tells Bellatrix, "You know how Ron is with the team? He does not focus on student learning; he focuses on fun. You have to talk to Hermione because we can't do anything about the gaps."

Scenario 4

The principal, Ben, is working to increase collaboration among the school's first-grade team members. Most of the team members have worked together for several years, making the implementation of new expectations difficult. One teacher, April, would prefer to close her door and continue with the status quo because her students typically pass. Leslie likes to do all the work and give weekly packets to other members. Tom enjoys the meetings because he likes the team he works with but is not too concerned with student progress. Ben knows they are not functioning at a high level, as student learning outcomes slowly decline and classroom management issues increase. However, they all get along so well that he wonders if addressing the problems is worth the trouble.

For each scenario, reflect on the questions in figure 4.5

As you worked through the scenarios, you probably noted some contrasting characteristics in both task or relationship orientation and identity.

- Hermione (task oriented; identity linked to work ethic) and Ron (relationship oriented; identity linked to being a good friend)
- Leslie (task oriented; identity linked to efficiency) and Tom (relationship oriented; identity linked to being engaged socially with others)
- Dwight (task oriented; identity linked to his work performance) and Jim (relationship oriented; identity linked to family)

Using the names of well-known characters helps participants visualize the scenario and understand how that person's strengths can also be their weakness; it also makes the conversation about characters instead of peers. When the conversation is about a scenario or a fictional character, people have a low-risk way to share their own strengths and weaknesses. For example, the "Hermiones" of the team can highlight that she gets the job done and solves problems while recognizing that she also gets easily flustered when other people do not understand immediately at a high level. It opens the door to being more self-aware and transparent.

Conclusion and Next Steps

This chapter focused on avoiding conflict spirals resulting from destructive conflicts, which can negatively affect task completion, relationships, and the overall function of the organization. After exploring the effects, it is critical to evaluate personal task or relationship orientation and identity to highlight the importance of self-awareness and understanding your peers to move conflict into a productive space. Equipped with knowledge, you moved from evaluating fictional scenarios to your own situations and worked through the process of understanding the motivations behind choices when in conflict.

Scenario	Label each character's tendency as either task oriented or relationship oriented.	Identify links to each character's identity. Who are they, and what might be their hot button?	How do a task or relationship orientation and identity contribute to conflict within the scenario?	Categorize the conflict.	What approach would you take to manage the conflict?
Scenario 1					
Scenario 2					
Scenario 3					
Scenario 4					

FIGURE 4.5: Conflict scenario reflection.

*Visit **go.SolutionTree.com/leadership** for a free reproducible version of this figure.*

Before you move on to the next chapter, think about conflicts you have experienced that have affected task completion, relationships, or the overall function of your team, department, campus, or district. Use the reproducible "Who Are We? Using Personal Orientation to Avoid Conflict Spirals" (page 103) to reflect. Look for your go-to orientation and identity hot buttons. It may be that you are leaning into your personal tendencies without exploring the usefulness of other tendencies and identities in different situations. Additionally, think about your coworkers and their go-to orientations and tendencies. All this information can help take the guesswork out of handling conflict effectively. Use the "Chapter 4 Next Steps: Avoiding Conflict Spirals" reproducible (page 105) to reflect on what you've learned about conflict spirals.

Task or Relationship Orientation?

Do you have a task orientation or a relationship orientation? Going down the list, circle the action that best describes you.

1.	I make the to-do list.	I make work fun.
2.	I keep us motivated.	I keep us on task.
3.	I make sure we concentrate on the work.	I make sure we explore everyone's ideas regarding the work.
4.	I make sure we get along.	I make sure we meet our timeline goals.
5.	I know the requirements of each team member.	I know what each team member needs.

See the charts that follow and answer the questions to reflect on your findings.

1. Which orientation do you lean toward?

____

____

____

____

____

____

2. Is your team more task oriented or relationship oriented?

____

____

____

____

____

____

3. How do similarities and differences in task and relationship orientation affect your team, campus, or district?

____

____

____

____

____

____

The circled actions indicate a task orientation.

1.	I make the to-do list.	I make work fun.
2.	I keep us motivated.	I keep us on task.
3.	I make sure we concentrate on the work.	I make sure we explore everyone's ideas regarding the work.
4.	I make sure we get along.	I make sure we meet our timeline goals.
5.	I know the requirements of each team member.	I know what each team member needs.

The circled actions indicate a relationship orientation.

1.	I make the to-do list.	I make work fun.
2.	I keep us motivated.	I keep us on task.
3.	I make sure we concentrate on the work.	I make sure we explore everyone's ideas regarding the work.
4.	I make sure we get along.	I make sure we meet our timeline goals.
5.	I know the requirements of each team member.	I know what each team member needs.

page 2 of 2

Who are We? Using Personal Orientation to Avoid Conflict Spirals

Think about three conflicts you have experienced that affected task completion, relationships, or the overall function of your team, department, campus, or district. Look for your go-to orientation and identity hot buttons. Additionally, think about your colleagues and their go-to orientations and tendencies. All this information can help take the guesswork out of handling conflict effectively.

Conflict Scenarios	How did your orientation and identity influence your role in the situation?	How did task or relationship orientation and identity impact the conflict in the situation?	What category was the conflict? How did you approach the conflict?
Scenario 1			
Scenario 2			
Scenario 3			

1. Which experiences ended in a productive conflict? Why? How did your choices lead to positive results?

2. Which experiences ended in a destructive conflict? Why? How did your choices lead to a conflict spiral?

3. Compare your results to those you work closely with. Then, compare with a person or group in a different role. What areas are similar, and what areas are different? Did anyone view a similar situation in a different way?

Chapter 4 Next Steps: Avoiding Conflict Spirals

Individually or with team members or colleagues, use the following questions to reflect on what you've learned about avoiding conflict spirals.

1. What are the effects of conflict on task completion?

2. What are the effects of conflict on relationships?

3. What are the effects of conflict on the overall function of the organization?

4. What is the task and relationship orientation of each person answering this question?

____

____

____

____

____

____

5. What are our hot-button issues? How can we regulate our responses to them?

____

____

____

____

____

____

6. Can we evaluate fictional and personal scenarios to determine the conflict category and possible conflict approach? Can we evaluate what decisions are more likely to lead to productive conflicts?

____

____

____

____

____

____

5

How Can We Keep Conflict Productive?

IMPROVING JOB SATISFACTION AND MOTIVATION

All employees bring strengths and weaknesses to the workplace. They also bring personal biases and external challenges from life outside the workplace, which colleagues are not always equipped to handle. It may seem as though job satisfaction and motivation are internal products linked to strengths and weaknesses, biases and challenges, but workplace conditions can be improved to increase job satisfaction and motivation. This chapter helps organizations create a work environment conducive to employee job satisfaction and motivation. Doing so leads to high-functioning teams able to weather the day-to-day storms of collaboration and interdependence (Ryan, Deci, Vansteenkiste, & Soenens, 2021).

At this point in our work to create a conflict-management plan, you are equipped to do the following.

- Establish clearly defined roles and responsibilities
- Categorize common conflicts
- Select an approach to manage the conflict
- Understand how personal tendencies and preferences affect conflicts and reduce conflict spirals

This chapter examines ways to improve job satisfaction and motivation using Self-Determination Theory (SDT; Deci & Ryan, 1985; Ryan & Deci, 2017). Adding in the component of SDT, which you'll learn more about in the next section, sets your organization up to build a strong comprehensive conflict-management plan where conflicts productively move everyone forward and employees feel fulfilled and driven to help all students learn at a high level.

In addition to SDT conditions, this chapter also explores how structures and responses can improve job satisfaction and motivation. The structures and responses build connections to the work in chapter 4 concerning task and relationship orientation. The end of the chapter looks back to scenarios from chapter 3 to see if we would revise our choices and thereby improve the SDT conditions.

Throughout this book, we have visited various Productive ISD campuses at the elementary, middle, and high school levels. Now, we will explore the district office and connect with some of the teams we have previously visited. No matter what role you currently serve, allow yourself a chance to think about other perspectives. Consider the challenges unique to every level and how educators can strive to improve the conditions through direct impact or simply by visualizing another person's perspective.

Self-Determination Theory

SDT is a framework for understanding human motivation, attributing job satisfaction to the fundamental SDT conditions of autonomy, competence, and relatedness (Deci & Ryan, 1985, Ryan & Deci, 2017). SDT also examines the dynamics of psychological needs within groups to support initiative and performance (Dysvik & Kuvaas, 2014). The world of education remains a people business. No matter the setup of your campus or district, individuals constantly move in groups—classrooms, grade-level teams, content-area teams, departments, and more.

SDT in education recognizes the innate need for maintaining a sense of self while also feeling as though you belong to a group (Ryan & Deci, 2002, 2017). We can see in the research that people experience higher levels of job satisfaction and motivation through SDT (Shim et al., 2022), but how does that relate to conflict? Once we understand the conditions and how they affect motivation, we can start to connect how each conflict-management decision affects the conditions.

This takes us back to the cyclical nature of conflict. Remember in chapter 4 how task and relationship conflict went hand in hand based on the trust we established with one another? The same is true with SDT when members of the organization lack motivation or do not gain satisfaction from their jobs. Student learning can suffer, teams can get locked into destructive conflict, or great teachers might leave the classroom.

In the context of education as related to conflict management, we use the following definitions for autonomy, competence, and relatedness.

- **Autonomy** is the condition that supports an individual's psychological needs in the workplace, described as a sense of ownership regarding one's behavior (Hobson & Maxwell, 2017; Kanat-Maymon, Elimelech, & Roth, 2020; Ryan et al., 2021; Szulawski, Kaźmierczak, & Prusik, 2021).
- **Competence** is the condition that supports an individual's psychological needs in the workplace, described as an individual's sense of efficacy or the feeling of having the ability to do one's job well (Hobson & Maxwell, 2017; Ryan et al., 2021; Szulawski et al., 2021).
- **Relatedness** is the condition that supports an individual's psychological needs in the workplace, described as a sense of belonging and adding value to an organization (Dysvik & Kuvaas, 2014; Hobson & Maxwell, 2017; Ryan et al., 2021; Szulawski et al., 2021).

Notice all three conditions refer to a feeling or sense. Perception becomes reality when working in groups; therefore, creating, maintaining, and improving the conditions give the sense or feeling of a better working environment. Working in educational settings presents challenges—it has always presented challenges. However, understanding the conditions of SDT can help organizations create an environment where individuals can focus on the positives and maintain the motivation to continue striving to improve student learning outcomes.

Now, let's dive into the three conditions to better understand why and how the conditions affect motivation and job satisfaction.

Autonomy

The topic of autonomy can be polarizing in school systems. So much of working within a system requires consensus and completing the job in the way that one person or one group determines best. However, the condition of autonomy within SDT challenges the negative connotation often connected with autonomy. Within SDT, autonomy means individuals can act in a way that matches their individual self, which does not equate to complete independence or the absence of a group (Ryan & Deci, 2002). As applied to education and school systems, autonomy is the feeling that individuals have the choice to respond to student needs or determine the best course of action that aligns with each individual self.

Think back to the conflict categories from chapter 2—curriculum differences, personality differences, and external pressures—and note how autonomy shows up in each area, from lesson planning to classroom management. People want to feel they have control over how to do their job, or they want to have a part in the decision-making process (Ryan & Deci, 2002). Either way, leaving employees without autonomy creates a culture of compliance where individuals struggle to stay motivated and enjoy their work. Psychologists Richard M. Ryan and Edward L. Deci (2002) make it clear that autonomy does not equate to complete compliance or conformity, but they also highlight that you can depend on others and still experience autonomy.

In general, school systems are built on protocols, procedures, and accountability measures that require sameness and compliance. Additionally, data drives instruction: If we see this number, we do *this*. If we see another number, we do *that*. In both scenarios, it is easy to see how creativity and innovation can be stifled, leading to compliance and complacency. It's not a pretty picture, which is why we must look for opportunities to establish, maintain, and improve autonomy within campuses and districts.

Here lies the hang-up in Productive ISD and campuses across the United States, Canada, and beyond. Autonomy can be painted in broad strokes with negative connotations, often equated with "going rogue." When district personnel work with some teams and campuses, they notice that the autonomy needs are the same from campus to campus, but trust in some teams remains higher than others. One kindergarten team at one campus has a team member who wants to try a different instructional strategy that stays true to the standard but might take a little extra instructional time, and campus leadership encourages the calculated risk, looking forward to seeing the results. However, another campus kindergarten team has asked for the same flexibility, and the campus leadership does not support it. Thus, the tension develops when the trust measures do not justify the relinquishment of control. However, working within the definition of autonomy as an SDT condition, the question becomes, "How will I know what someone has to offer if I never let them have any choice or voice related to their work? Additionally, what are we losing in motivation and job satisfaction by reducing autonomy?"

As the district personnel work with all teams, they see how levels of autonomy vary from campus to campus, but they also notice that the campus leaders are not always wrong in their assessment of which teams are prepared for autonomy and which are not. While schools with proven student learning results might need to explore different instructional strategies or streamline required paperwork that has become a matter of compliance, other schools or teams may not be ready for less oversight and more independence.

It is important to note that balance and moderation can create conditions where people have some ownership of their work. Evaluate the variables and look for opportunities to increase autonomy. Avoid being in complete control or allowing complete autonomy. Strike a balance and do not shy away from teaching people the expectations and then releasing them to get there in a manner that makes sense to them. Find places (preferably places that do not have legislation attached) to innovate.

When campuses and districts have new staff or capacity needs improvement, autonomy may temporarily suffer; this is a difficult truth that must be accepted and accounted for when addressing conflict. Conflict will develop when people feel they must comply without staying true to their own opinions, but when someone learns a new position or struggles with having the capacity to complete the job, less autonomy might be the best choice. Imagine a district instructional coach working with a new teacher. The coach will probably choose to be rigid about teaching essential standards, incorporating best practices, and using data-driven instruction. This will be necessary, but it will also affect the condition of autonomy. If the lack of autonomy continues for too long, the teacher might feel less motivated and satisfied.

If you just shouted "Amen!" because you feel like a lack of autonomy is stifling you, keep reading before highlighting the entire paragraph and taking it to your next book study meeting. This is a necessary part of the process. There is freedom in the form. Once people are well-versed in the rigors of their jobs and can lead a classroom or group with fidelity, then leadership can revisit increasing autonomy;

we do not know whether we are well-versed in what our job entails and successfully leading a classroom or team until we see student results.

We want to improve the condition of autonomy continuously. Balancing this need with ensuring proper alignment throughout the district requires reflection, especially for those in campus or district leadership positions. Look at the health of the teaching staff *and* student results. And look at *all* student results, not just those who historically perform well; look at growth for every student. Going back to the kindergarten teams, the district staff notes that beginning-of-year data points to a need for more time on foundational skills. In the past, students at most elementary campuses within Productive ISD came to kindergarten with a strong knowledge of letter sounds. However, the kindergartners at Challenge Elementary arrived with mixed background knowledge. Based on this data, the district staff commits to working with the kindergarten team to respond to student need and provide support as needed. Without the autonomy to respond to changes in student needs, student learning for the current kindergarten class would be affected.

Autonomy appropriately incorporated to benefit students and teachers shows up in teacher retention *and* student progress results. If there is too much flexibility too fast, individuals and groups may not be equipped to respond appropriately, resulting in lower levels of student learning. And when evidence of student learning decreases, the potential for higher levels of conflict within groups increases. However, if the hold is too tight for too long, the compliance culture may produce short-term results but job satisfaction, motivation, and innovation may suffer.

Competence

The second condition that supports an individual's psychological needs in the workplace is competence, the individual's sense of efficacy or the feeling of having the ability to do one's job well (Hobson & Maxwell, 2017; Ryan et al., 2021; Szulawski et al., 2021). Competence and autonomy work together synergistically and can even increase intrinsic motivation when employees take ownership of their competence (Dysvik & Kuvaas, 2014; Ryan et al., 2021). Notice the wording of competence as an SDT condition. The perception of ability becomes paramount to the process of improving the competence condition.

Competence, capacity, and efficacy share similar definitions within the context of education and can yield positive learning results for students and teachers. John Hattie (2016) rates teacher efficacy as the number-one influence on improving student learning outcomes. However, improving the competence of individuals and teams has more layers (five, to be exact) because competence as an SDT condition relies on the perception of individuals as capable of being successful at their job. In the following sections, I explain each of the five layers in detail: (1) moving between roles and responsibilities, (2) taking on tasks with higher difficulty, (3) shifting from task to task, (4) adding new responsibilities, and (5) changing the level of functioning.

1. Moving Between Roles and Responsibilities

In the first layer, competence can increase and decrease constantly as individuals move fluidly between roles and responsibilities. The Productive ISD curriculum and instruction team experiences the fluidity of competence daily. Imani, one of the specialists, spent most of her classroom years at the elementary level, specifically the third and fourth grades. When she works with elementary teachers, Imani often feels confident in her ability to add value to any task that comes her way. However, she feels the tension of conflict with the first-grade team at ABC Elementary. The pushback generally relates to foundational literacy skills, which Imani has extensive experience with. Even though she has an impressive résumé, the team challenges Imani's ability to truly understand the rigors of teaching foundational literacy skills because she did not specifically teach first grade.

To overcome some of the tension, Imani often volunteers to help with small groups. Each time she works directly with students, she notes that the team's trust in her competence grows. What Imani initially considered a personality conflict or petty difference was actually rooted in care for student learning. The "specialist" title did not equate to competence from the team's perspective. Imani recognized that she would need to build trust to decrease conflict over her approach.

2. Taking on Tasks With Higher Difficulty

A second layer emerges with different tasks and the perceived level of difficulty. Competence substantially influences performance, especially when tasks are not too hard or too easy. Think about the times when you have struggled to get started with a task. Or put yourself in a student's shoes and think about writing an essay, working through a difficult calculus problem, or speaking to a peer in Spanish. If you ask a team of teachers in the English department to write an essay, they will probably feel competent enough to start and quickly complete the task. However, motivation may wane if you ask the same individuals to work on a calculus problem or read an essay in Spanish to a peer. The same people who are competent with the first task (writing an essay) might feel completely ill-equipped with the other tasks (calculus and Spanish). If the English teachers refuse to try the calculus problem, does that make them incompetent, even though they excelled at the writing task?

Additionally, while some of the English teachers might struggle when trying to complete the calculus or Spanish tasks, others might have skills in those areas, which would change their perceived level of task difficulty. This can impact the potential for conflict. When part of the team feels they have the ability to take on the task and the other part feels completely out of their depth, it can affect the team dynamics. This is why it is crucial to evaluate the situations people are in before labeling anyone incompetent. Remember that when tension feels personal, the conflict potential increases and tends to spiral faster. Members of the organization can maintain competence when they focus on adjusting and scaffolding the task while building the capacity to handle more challenging responsibilities.

The same is true when a task is too easy. For example, making copies for people is my love language, so I am always the first to volunteer, but some collaborative teams give copy duty to the new teacher. That might be fine if the new teacher loves copies as much as I do, but many times, the copy person starts to lose motivation and job satisfaction if they are not being challenged. A new teacher may need significant help building the capacity to give strong feedback to students or manage classroom transitions; consider how you can improve competence in these areas before simply assigning copy duty for the year.

One way to improve new teacher competence is to take advantage of fresh eyes. In many respects, the new teacher is the most prepared to identify blind spots. If a college-educated professional cannot understand the assessment rubric or find a connection between the learning target and the lesson, adjustments probably need to be made. If a new teacher or team uncovers Tier 1 instructional needs before the initial instruction, they can adjust accordingly, reducing intervention and increasing extension requirements. The new teacher has just helped the group improve student learning outcomes through increased collaboration. The next time they are asked to contribute to unit planning, the conditions are improved for buy-in to complete the task. Improved content capacity is the byproduct of putting a new teacher in a stretch position instead of defaulting to an easier task. Evaluating a unit plan to find areas for improvement requires thinking through and visualizing how the different pieces will come together. The new teacher is competent to complete the task when given the voice to freely share insights only held by fresh eyes.

3. Shifting From Task to Task

At the third layer, our levels of competence can fluctuate throughout the day as we move from task to task or even class to class. Remember that competence relies on feeling capable, and feelings can be fleeting! Peter, the director of student services for Productive ISD, experiences this layer when working with assistant principals throughout the district. He notices that a particular high school assistant principal, Brendan, consistently does well with safety-related and operational tasks. Brendan submits all paperwork on time and implements difficult safety protocols with ease. He also does well with evaluating teachers of tested subjects. However, Brendan struggles when working with career and technical education (CTE) and fine arts teachers. Although the work he does with other teachers consistently improves learning outcomes, Brendan does not feel that he has the same credibility with CTE and fine arts teachers. The negative perception he has about his competence leads to wavering feelings of competence from task to task. Peter notes this perception issue and looks for ways to build Brendan's capacity and confidence in working with all teachers.

4. Adding New Responsibilities

A fourth layer is that competence fluctuates when people move into a different role with new responsibilities. Most teacher leaders, administrators, counselors, and instructional coaches began their careers as teachers and then transitioned to those other roles throughout their careers. Each time a move occurs, it can affect competence. Part of the transition takes us back to gaining clarity on the role and identifying responsibilities for the new role: "Do I truly understand what the role requires and how to effectively complete the job tasks?" Furthermore, the role can often come without an official contract or title change, which can affect a person's perception of their competence.

For example, a teacher, Sinitta, moves into a department chair position. The new role does not change Sinitta's contract, and she still actively teaches alongside other teachers. Sinitta shows high levels of competence in teaching, but this is her first time being an intermediary between teams and administrators. The change requires a new skill set packed with complex relationship dynamics. Sinitta must balance the need for task completion and relationships to maintain trust and continued productivity. The capacity required to achieve the balance did not emerge in her past role as a teacher. Sinitta felt completely competent in teaching, but she struggles to feel immediately confident in the department chair role.

5. Changing the Level of Functioning

A fifth and final layer involves how changing a team's or campus's level of functioning impacts competence. If your role change means going from a work environment that was not healthy and collaborative to one with a high-functioning team or campus, you will face a learning curve, especially if you are moving into an administrative position. Leading strong functioning groups without experience as a member will present challenges for parts of the job. For example, your competence may shine in helping teachers with classroom management, but you may need help understanding how grade-level teams come together to ensure high levels of learning for all students. When faced with those obstacles, find solid resources to learn from and observe the learning in action. Always remember that healthy organizations foster learning for adults and students. What begins as a gap in capacity can grow into a strength.

As with moving into an administrative role, teachers moving into team facilitator, team leader, or department chair roles may have an adjustment period while transitioning into a role with new complexities. The various teacher leader roles place a person squarely between their peers and administration. Carrying out the administration's directives while building relationships and trust within a team challenges the most experienced teacher leader. However, it can be a competence crippler for a new teacher leader, especially if the new person has not spent time learning within a high-functioning collaborative team.

In Productive ISD, Dariush, one of the curriculum directors, is a whiz at instructional technology and other various responsibilities within his role, but he was a shining star within a toxic environment. Dariush's background did not include many opportunities for healthy collaboration with other professionals. Thus, he lacks understanding of why grade-level teams want to align and work together. He has always relied on individual competence, so he often leans on other directors to learn more about collaboration and how to bring people together instead of flying solo. By collaborating with other directors to improve competence, Dariush gives himself constant opportunities for practice within a safe space. Then he applies the lessons in his work with campuses throughout the district. The loop of learning and practice helps Dariush improve his confidence while accelerating his progress and maintaining his motivation to continue the loop.

Relatedness

Relatedness, the third condition supporting an individual's psychological needs in the workplace, describes the sense of belonging and adding value to an organization

(Dysvik & Kuvaas, 2014; Hobson & Maxwell, 2017; Ryan et al., 2021; Szulawski et al., 2021). The feeling of being cared for and connected to others or the absence of that feeling can directly affect employee effectiveness and success. Research points to the importance of a collegial environment (Klein et al., 2018), but the difficulty lies in implementing programs and processes to increase relatedness.

District office employees from Productive ISD recognize the importance of a collegial environment, but they find it difficult to create and foster a sense of belonging. They are constantly trying to navigate complex relationships and serve in the middleman role between district and campus overlap. Specifically, the special education department tries to help by auditing required paperwork to catch clerical errors or inconsistencies. Some campuses appreciate the help; other campuses, however, feel the special education department staff do not appreciate how budget cuts have affected them. They make comments like the following.

- "Maybe they should come work with us for a week and see how many *T*'s they forget to cross."
- "We are drowning in paperwork, referrals, and student needs, but they don't know that because they only see us forgetting to check a box on screen 11 to make the modified curriculum information visible."
- "Engage with me face to face before you judge my work from your office."

Yikes! The special education department staff wanted to help by taking something off the loaded plates of others. However, without relatedness, people struggle to receive the help they need with a positive perspective.

Any time leaders can create opportunities for staff members to interact, learn, and collaborate with others, chances are that relatedness will increase. Relatedness centers on trust, and trust is required for staff members to come to the table with vulnerability to do the difficult work of improving student learning and progress for all students. Knowing this, one would think we should simply value one another and create a sense of belonging, which would lead to strong bonds of trust capable of weathering conflict. Easy, right? Unfortunately, the process of building trust and increasing relatedness cannot be artificially created or accelerated.

Sometimes you might not even like the people you work with, but you still must meet with them weekly and make choices together that affect your classroom or your role. And therein lies the key: Relatedness does not hinge on likability, but building collegiality can lead to greater respect and trust. This is another place where cycles can create positive or negative conditions. If you are not my cup of tea, but we have established trust between us, a positive feeling of relatedness can flourish, creating a positive cycle. However, without relatedness, trust continues to erode with each small conflict, creating a negative cycle.

Relatedness strongly affects conflict, job satisfaction, and motivation. When we embed solid systems into daily work, we cannot lose our humanity. People come together every day to improve student outcomes. Those people, from bottom to top, deserve to walk into their job feeling that they hold value and belong. When we can achieve that goal, refinement and growth become less difficult. If you trust someone and they ask to help you improve your content knowledge, you are more likely to agree. Even better, with established relatedness bonds, people are more likely to initiate the conversation and ask for help when feeling as though they are not equipped for a task.

Ways to Improve the Three SDT Conditions

When organizations work to establish, maintain, and improve the three conditions of SDT, job satisfaction and motivation grow (Ryan & Deci, 2000). Autonomy, competence, and relatedness are vital within every role in every school system (Hobson & Maxwell, 2017) because all three conditions connect deeply to each other. It is difficult to trust someone when you question their competence. If someone questions your competence, why would you want to build a relationship with that person? The same is true when considering autonomy. If I have provided the opportunity for you to take ownership of a task and you did not follow through, it would be hard for me to think that you can tackle another task with similar difficulty.

One helpful way to improve the three conditions is to consider structures and responses. *Structures* set up environments conducive to improving the three conditions and relate to task completion. *Responses* set up ways to use relationships to improve the conditions. The following sections review both approaches.

Structures

Referring back to chapter 4, think about the people who lean toward a task-completion orientation. Remember that these are the people who help get the job done, and they will need structures in place to keep the organization moving forward. Much of the structural work will fall to campus administrative teams and district staff as they divide time and other resources to improve autonomy, competence, and relatedness. Ask yourself these questions.

- "Do people have time dedicated to collaborating and responding to student needs?"
- "Do people know which responsibilities are flexible and which responsibilities are non-negotiable?"
- "Do people have opportunities to develop professionally?"
- "Is professional development differentiated based on experience and need?"
- "Do staff have opportunities to build trust and relationships throughout the year?"
- "Does time or resource allocation hinder relatedness among teachers, teams, or campuses?"

Although the structural issues in these questions may be administrators' responsibilities, teachers can also use the questions to examine their own department and classrooms. The questions can also help teachers articulate what might help or hinder the three conditions. We will dig into more about structures in chapter 6.

Responses

Referring to chapter 4, think about the people who lean toward a relationship orientation. Remember that these are the people who help build community, and they need trusting relationships in place to keep the organization moving forward. The way we respond to each other matters, especially when trying to improve relatedness. Ask yourself these questions.

- "Do people know how to navigate difficult conversations?"
- "Do we feel comfortable enough with each other to disagree?"
- "Are we equipped to vocalize our feelings without it becoming an attack?"
- "How are we responding—directly, indirectly, passive aggressively, indifferently, or avoidantly?"

I listen to teachers and administrators respond to student issues with so much kindness and care every single day, but can I be honest? I then hear the same people respond to each other with a lack of care for their coworkers' humanity. I am guilty of this as well. Sometimes I have an infinite amount of grace for students but not my colleagues or myself.

One of the ways to learn how to respond well to others and have difficult conversations without destroying relationships is to consider maintaining and improving autonomy, competence, and relatedness. When choosing how to respond to others, ask yourself the following questions.

- "Will my response take away a person's sense of ownership?"
- "Will my response take away a person's sense of ability?"
- "Will my response take away a person's sense of belonging?"

We want the answer to be *no*, but once again, let's be honest. Sometimes we will purposefully make a choice to lower autonomy for a good reason. In that situation, we need to consider how we can increase one of the other conditions. Maybe we will increase the time spent mentoring that person to build trust and connection. Responding well involves recognizing the ebb and flow of the conditions and meeting people where they are in their journey to continuous improvement. After all, the goal of using the SDT conditions is to increase the probability of productive conflict and reduce the probability of destructive conflict.

Scenarios for Reflection: Improving Conditions

The scenarios in chapter 3 allowed for rich discussions within teams, departments, campuses, and districts about the choices that might lead to positive outcomes when considering the type of conflicts. Now, we will revisit those scenarios to see if the choices we made in chapter 3 would stay the same. Consider how your choices can maintain or improve autonomy, competence, and relatedness.

Scenario 1

The science instructional coach assists several teams across Productive ISD. He has a positive rapport with most of the collaborative teams and individual campus administration teams. One campus, however, seems focused on compliance instead of commitment. That team checks all the necessary boxes, but many of the decisions they make together do not authentically impact each classroom. The instructional coach wants the team to dive into the standards together and use data to respond to current student needs, but the team members fear conflict may occur if they hash it out. They are happy with the status quo and push back whenever the instructional coach guides them away from superficially addressing lesson planning instead of digging deeper.

Scenario 2

After looking at an upcoming unit assessment, the algebra team at Platinum High School decides they need to adjust the number of questions on each standard to match what they have deemed essential and plan to monitor throughout the unit. Each member of the four-person team agrees to write two questions for their assigned standard. The team makeup includes two experienced teachers who have been on the algebra team for five years, one experienced teacher new to the algebra team, and one first-year teacher who completed his student teaching with the team the previous year. At the next meeting, one person—one of the experienced teachers—does not have their questions ready. The team facilitator is shocked that an experienced teacher isn't prepared, but the new teacher has two questions ready. The lack of preparation from an experienced teacher concerns the team facilitator.

Scenario 3

Although the IB film studies teachers are singletons at each high school campus in Productive ISD, their students take a district common assessment two to three times per year. The IB coordinator for the district finds these check-ins help guide the teachers' instructional strategies and improve success rates on the IB tests. During the last collaborative meeting, the teachers agreed on specific protocols for testing to ensure valid and reliable results. Unfortunately, although two teachers followed the protocol, two teachers did not. The IB coordinator typically tracks the results and can predict success rates based on the common assessments; however, the skewed results present a problem.

For each scenario, reflect on the questions in figure 5.1 (page 122).

Scenario	Reflect on each condition (autonomy, competence, and relatedness) to determine which conditions might currently be affected.	What would you change or add to your decisions from chapter 3? Why?	What do you anticipate will be the positive outcomes of your revised choices?	What do you anticipate will be the drawbacks of your revised choices?
Scenario 1				
Scenario 2				
Scenario 3				

FIGURE 5.1: Improving conditions scenario reflection.

Visit ***go.SolutionTree.com/leadership*** *for a free reproducible version of this figure.*

Conclusion and Next Steps

This chapter focused on the SDT conditions of autonomy, competence, and relatedness. Understanding the effects of SDT conditions on motivation helps us manage conflict within our campuses and districts so that it is productive rather than destructive. SDT conditions vary depending on their facilitation within an environment; therefore, the needs of autonomy, competence, and relatedness are not traits we possess but rather environmental factors we can optimize. As a result, the environment that school leaders and teams foster and maintain either enables or impedes the attainment of those needs (Lee, Nie, & Bai, 2020; Power & Goodnough, 2019). We can help improve these conditions through structures and responses that encourage task completion and relationship building.

Use the reproducible "How Can We Keep Conflict Productive? Creating Conditions to Improve Job Satisfaction and Motivation" (page 124) to organize the conflict type, management tendency, and possible affected conditions to plan the best choice. Think about conflict situations you face often in your role or revisit some of the conflicts you explored in previous chapters. For each conflict situation, continue to look for ways in your action plan to proactively maintain the conditions of autonomy, competence, and relatedness. Then, reflect on the results and ripple effects of the decisions. Use the "Chapter 5 Next Steps: Improving Conditions and Motivation" reproducible (page 127) to reflect on what you've learned about improving conditions and motivation.

How Can We Keep Conflict Productive? Creating Conditions to Improve Job Satisfaction and Motivation

Use this tool to organize the conflict type, management tendency, and possible affected conditions for planning. Think about conflict situations you face often in your role or revisit some of the conflicts you explored in previous chapters. For each conflict situation, continue to look for ways in your action plan to proactively maintain the conditions of autonomy, competence, and relatedness. Then, reflect on the results and ripple effects of the decisions in the questions that follow the table.

Situation	Type of Conflict	Management Tendency	Effects	Action Plan
Example: Data shows that second-grade student learning progress in mathematics has decreased in the last nine weeks. The second-grade team analyzes the data together and discovers two teachers show significant growth; one teacher's growth is stagnant, and one teacher shows a decline.	Curriculum, specifically categorized as dealing with instruction delivery and intervention	Our team tends to lean into demographic differences instead of tackling the issue. We absorb the conflict so that people's feelings are not hurt.	The two teachers showing growth take on more work to overcome deficits. During flex time, they always take the students who are struggling. They typically reteach lessons during this time just to make sure all students get the essential concepts. Our avoidance of the issue is causing burnout, and frustration levels are high. When the teacher with declining progress offers suggestions, others tend to ignore those ideas—even when those ideas have value.	1. We need to come together as a team and determine—based on data—what specific learning targets are strengths and weaknesses for each class. 2. We need to determine what special populations show strengths and weaknesses within each learning target and class. 3. We will be open and transparent about strategy success and failure. 4. The teachers showing significant growth will incorporate more modeling within team meetings. To offset the extra time spent modeling, the team will determine ways to reallocate various tasks.

Situation	Type of Conflict	Management Tendency	Effects	Action Plan
Situation:				
Situation:				
Situation:				

1. What conditions are improving as we follow the action plan?

2. What structures and responses should we consider within the situations?

3. Compare your results to those of colleagues you work closely with. Then, compare with a person or group in a different role. What areas are similar, and what areas are different? Did anyone view a similar situation in a different way?

Chapter 5 Next Steps: Improving Conditions and Motivation

Individually or with team members or colleagues, use the following questions to reflect on what you've learned about the Self-Determination Theory (SDT) conditions of autonomy, competence, and relatedness.

1. What is the current state of the three SDT conditions in our school or district?

2. What are the effects of the conditions on job satisfaction and motivation?

3. How can structures and responses increase or decrease the conditions?

4. How does the content in this chapter about autonomy, competence, and relatedness support the content in previous chapters?

____

____

____

____

____

5. After evaluating a conflict, what steps should we take to create an action plan for improving autonomy, competence, and relatedness?

____

____

____

____

____

6

What Can We Be Proactive About?

IMPLEMENTING STRUCTURES FOR SUCCESS

Most of the book up to this point has been a combination of research and practice, but this chapter leans into setting up teams, departments, campuses, and districts for success. Managing conflict largely relies on responding in the appropriate manner to the situation at hand. There is no one-size-fits-all, step-by-step approach for managing conflict in schools. That is why it is necessary to create a comprehensive conflict-management plan to effectively navigate the complex conflicts that happen daily in organizations.

In this chapter, we revisit some of the structures touched on throughout the book for understanding and making productive use of conflict. Here, we focus on understanding how the structure and logistics of organizations directly affect potential conflicts. The journey started in chapter 1 with the unpacking of roles and responsibilities; now we will go deeper into the structures people operate in, exploring the following topics.

- Mission, vision, values, and goals
- Agendas
- Norms
- Meeting structures
- Resource allocation

- Scheduling
- Leadership teams
- Training
- Curriculum
- Responses to systemic issues

Within each topic, our focus is on what we can control within our context to proactively address possible conflicts. Each piece offers potential ways to address structural issues causing conflict. This can be a starting point for your organization to shape a system that works for your context.

Mission, Vision, Values, and Goals

When organizations haven't taken the time to articulate why they exist, who they want to be, and where they want to go, campus or district initiatives often fall flat. Establishing the campus and district mission, vision, values, and goals creates structural alignment within the organization. More than words on paper or a catchphrase on a staff T-shirt, the mission, vision, values, and goals tell individuals within the system what matters to the organization and why.

The most appropriate guide for defining and establishing the mission, vision, values, and goals for a campus or district comes from the PLC at Work® process (DuFour et al., 2024; DuFour, DuFour, Eaker, Mattos, & Muhammad, 2021).

- **Mission** refers to our purpose: Why do we exist?
- **Vision** refers to our future: What do we hope to become?
- **Values** refers to our collective commitments: How must we act to achieve our vision?
- **Goals** refers to our targets: How will we measure progress?

Understanding these definitions is the first step, but alignment occurs with greater fidelity when the members of the organization believe in the mission and act to achieve the purpose. Alignment protects the organization from conflicts caused by structural confusion.

In Productive ISD, the district administration provides the mission and vision statements to schools. At Discovery Middle School, most teachers do not know what the statements say, much less believe in the statements. Principal Munson sees how the lack of organizational direction causes unnecessary conflicts due to misalignment. He always considered academic and character development to be the mission of the school. However, several conflicts occurred the previous year between the teachers over which curricular subjects were tested and which weren't. The teachers of tested subjects made it clear that they felt more time and money should be spent helping them bolster student achievement, which the state measures based on standardized tests.

If the mission hinges on achievement, the teachers of the subjects being tested might have a valid point. If this is our purpose, we should spend more time and money to pursue that purpose. The teachers of the subjects not being tested thought the mission centered on developing students in all academics and character, which would mean all subjects carry equal value and all subjects should focus on both academic and character development, not just higher test scores.

The campus instructional leadership team, consisting of teacher leaders and key staff members, meets once or twice a month to check in, address campus needs, and communicate key information. Principal Munson decides to use a portion of this time over four or five sessions to evaluate the current mission and vision. Once the instructional leadership team develops an initial starting point for the mission and vision, the entire staff will work to finalize the mission and vision before creating the values and goals. Principal Munson wants to maintain consistency in the mission, vision, and values while adjusting the goals each year to meet the needs of the current students and staff. Incorporating the leadership team and staff into the process increases the probability of buy-in, which will also increase the potential for alignment. When people participate in the process, they gain clarity around the structure and expectations. With clarity, potential conflicts can stay productive.

Agendas

You may be wondering how an agenda can lessen conflict. Agendas can truly make or break meeting success, and when meetings become unproductive or chaotic, tensions arise. Creating an agenda involves advanced planning and provides time to consider how much you can accomplish in the allotted amount of time (LeBlanc & Nosik, 2019). A well-planned agenda of items to accomplish during the scheduled meeting honors people's time, and communicating the plan in advance of the meeting helps people prepare any necessary materials or questions

(LeBlanc & Nosik, 2019). Planning lowers the potential for wasted time, and communicating lowers the risk of someone being caught off guard.

Think back to Anthony, the English teacher at Discovery Middle School, and his use of the agenda to reduce conflict. Principal Munson notes that the English department excels at structuring agendas to serve the team well. Purposeful with clear expectations for time, the agenda spelled out Anthony's needs while also respecting the team's time. Anthony addressed group items during the meeting and kept individual questions for after the team meeting conclusion. How many times have you sat in a meeting and felt frustration due to wasted time or too much time focused on individual questions? Agendas matter because they guide meetings and lessen the chances of the meeting going awry.

Principal Munson noted that the English department experiences less departmental conflict, but the social studies team struggles with task completion conflict. He decides to assess their agenda structures and see if he can identify any adjustments to reduce team conflict. Figure 6.1 shows the social studies department agenda, and figure 6.2 shows the English department agenda.

Social Studies Department Meeting Agenda

October Meeting

1. Celebrations
2. Campus updates
3. Upcoming events
4. Questions and concerns

FIGURE 6.1: Social studies department meeting agenda.

As you review both agendas, use the following questions to determine similarities and differences between them.

1. What similarities do you notice between the two agendas?
2. What differences do you notice between the two agendas?
3. What conflicts might develop or be lessened based on your agenda observations?

English Department Meeting Agenda

October Meeting, 2:45 p.m. to 3:15 p.m.

1. Norms review (1–2 minutes)
   - We honor each other's time by starting and ending meetings on time.
   - We preview the agenda and prepare any questions for the appropriate time in the meeting.
   - We determine whether a question pertains to the entire group and save individual questions for another time.
   - We assume positive intentions with all group members and voice our opinions with respect to others.
   - We capture opportunities for learning and consistently reflect on our contribution to overall department success.
2. Celebrations (3–5 minutes)
3. Campus and department updates (5–8 minutes)
   - Essay writing
     - Where is each grade level with scaffolding at the close of the first nine-week grading period?
   - PSAT testing
     - Information regarding proctors and schedules
     - Eighth-grade students only, but additional teachers and staff are involved
4. Upcoming events (5–8 minutes)
   - Professional development day on Election Day
     - Information regarding schedules and expectations
5. Questions and concerns (3–5 minutes)
   - Instructional leadership team meeting next week. Any questions?
6. Meeting wrap-up (1–2 minutes)

FIGURE 6.2: English department meeting agenda.

Principal Munson notes that the English department agenda provides more details and direction to guide the team through the required items. The maximum time ranges add up to the total time of the meeting, so the team can adjust if one segment takes longer than planned. The agenda does contain a lot of detail, which makes Principal Munson wonder if the length could be overwhelming. He asks Yolanda, the department chair, and she tells him that the structure works best for the department meetings because they do not meet every week. Yolanda states that grade-level team meetings use a slightly different agenda structure because there are fewer people and the meetings are more frequent.

Principal Munson discusses some possible agenda improvements with Tony, the social studies department chair. He encourages including time ranges and bullet points to maintain a productive flow and increase clarity. Tony agrees that the agenda tweaks can improve productivity and lessen conflict. The last few social studies team meetings have been a cacophony of voices and closed with more questions than answers. Team members are leaving frustrated and without clarity, but the changes will help.

Norms

Similar to agendas, norms can be an afterthought or compliance piece that gets overlooked if individuals do not understand why the structure reduces conflicts. Formal team norms can increase a group's problem-solving potential (Taggar & Ellis, 2007), equipping teams and departments to better handle conflicts. The first step in creating norms helps groups offset weaknesses with a norm to check their behavior. Think about the activities to get to know each other and explore how identity influences hot buttons from chapter 4. These same exercises, along with other personality assessments, can help groups to talk about strengths and weaknesses in a low-risk way. The information these exercises provide can create strong norms because the exercises proactively tackle tensions before they begin.

For example, while creating norms at the beginning of the year, a team member expresses that they struggle with timeliness and will need a norm that addresses that personal weakness. Another team member states they are always on time and never struggle with deadlines, but they tend to miss group stress cues and unintentionally hurt people's feelings. In both situations, the team member presents a personal weakness and proposes a norm to improve accountability. If the issue emerges throughout the year, the team will feel better equipped to initiate the accountability conversation because the person offered it up. Any time we independently decide to elicit assistance and improve performance, future conversations become easier. Correction does not feel like a personal attack because we asked for the help.

Once the group creates its initial norms, getting into the habit of reviewing norms each meeting also lowers conflict potential. If the team waits to revisit or review the norms after a conflict begins, it feels like a personal indictment. For example, a random inclusion of norms review might cause a team member to ask, "Why are we suddenly talking about honoring each other's time on the day that I showed up two minutes late? They never recognize how hard I try to be on time, but today I was finishing up a parent phone call." Conversely, reviewing norms regularly sets the tone that every meeting begins the same, and these standards help us to be effective regardless of weaknesses. It is not personal; it is simply a constant reminder of the commitments we make to each other.

Meeting Structures

We covered some of the structures within meetings that can help lower destructive conflict, but the who, when, and where of meetings can also influence conflict. Being proactive and deciding the meeting structures in advance help people feel safe in the situation. That psychological safety begins with trust that the meeting structures support a culture of learning and growing through risk taking, not a random evaluation or "gotcha" (Frazier, Fainshmidt, Klinger, Pezeshkan, & Vracheva, 2017).

The people who attend a meeting may be mandated at the campus or district level. An administrator or instructional coach may attend every meeting or pop in as needed. Both ways can work, but being proactive about the choice is pivotal to reducing destructive conflict. If a group expects an administrator or instructional coach to attend meetings sporadically but they suddenly attend every meeting, the perception will be that the team is having trouble.

Picking a meeting time and sticking to it as often as possible includes making sure that attendees have minimal schedule conflicts. This structural choice increases consistency and helps meeting attendees plan their schedules accordingly. Consider everything from coach and sponsor practice schedules to common dates for other meetings. Additionally, anticipate possible months when meeting times may need to be adjusted, including testing season.

The meeting space can also influence conflict. Sometimes, if there are no other available options, meetings may take place in a teacher's room or administrator's office. However, when you have a choice, a neutral area can balance power differentials and improve collaboration (Hocker et al., 2022; van Bunderen et al., 2018).

Resource Allocation

Time and money continually emerge as conflict inducers (van Bunderen et al., 2018). Resource allocation affects many aspects of the school system daily, but let's examine resource allocation as a structural component. Money allocation differs from state to state, province to province, and district to district. Since the rules of spending frequently fall under federal, state, and provincial mandates, we will focus on time as a resource more likely to be controllable. Time as a structural component typically presents in the master schedule and meeting schedules. This structure usually falls on the shoulders of administration teams, both at the campus and district levels, although teachers also determine the best ways to allocate time to lessen stress and lower tensions.

Dr. Rawlins, the principal at Platinum High School, works tirelessly with the administrative team to create a master schedule that provides for common time within teams and departments. The team tries its best to place teacher conference periods together, but some teachers teach two different subjects, and others have different responsibilities that require different time allocations. Time challenges exist every year, but the administrative team noted fewer problems when they implemented two helpful structures linked to a staff survey.

First, the administrative team surveys the staff at the end of each year to gain insight into personal preferences, areas of structural strengths, and areas of structural weaknesses. The survey has resulted in several staff-suggested improvements and innovations. The administration team uses time in the summer to read through each survey with the Self-Determination Theory conditions of autonomy, competence, and relatedness in mind. Think back to chapter 5 and the ways improving SDT conditions can influence job satisfaction and motivation. The administrative team will never make everyone happy; resources are limited, and difficult decisions about allocation must be made. But knowing the team listens to the staff and is actively improving conditions matters greatly to the staff.

The survey itself heightens staff's sense of autonomy, as they feel their voices matter. The tweaks and changes based on the survey improve staff perception that every individual controls at least a portion of the way things are done. The survey also improves competence, as staff perceive their abilities go beyond instruction. Staff point out blind spots to the administrative team, exposing matters that increase tension and conflict but do not immediately pop out to the administrative team.

For example, in response to one of the survey questions, one teacher brought up the frustration of having the same planning period every year. Her planning period has fallen during second period for the last five years, while one of her friends from another department has had fourth period. The administrative team wonders at first why this would be an issue. As they read the commentary, they find that official attendance takes place during fourth period. The friend gets extra time in the form of less paperwork. What some might regard as insignificant continues to erode a staff member's morale and relatedness with a colleague. Another survey commenter expressed frustration at always having first-period planning because he felt he lost valuable time helping substitutes, and yet another calls attention to being scheduled with her elective subject when she would prefer to have common time with the tested subject team.

Based on the feedback, the team started looking at ways to shuffle the master schedule from year to year to mix it up. Team members could also incorporate at least some of the staff preferences or explain why they were not able to consider the preference based on other constraints. The counselors indicated that it was helpful to know the teachers' preferences as they worked with the administrative team on the master schedules as well. Instead of arbitrarily placing classes on the scheduling board and then clicking the button to assign students into classes, they could see the human side of how scheduling matters to people. The staff felt heard and appreciated.

The second positive outcome from the survey emerged from the suggested innovations. One teacher suggested that a narrow hallway with considerable congestion was causing students to fight. Her frustration centered on trying to monitor the hallway and students entering her classroom effectively. The school officer and assistant principal evaluated the monitoring plan, seeing that two possible fixes might improve the situation. First, the assistant principal would move from the open common space to the hallway, alternating between even and odd periods each day for the first week. If the issue improves because of active monitoring, they will look at resource allocation and figure out if it is feasible to have someone there each period or more sporadically throughout the day. If that does not help the issue, their other possible fix is to make the hallway single direction to improve the flow and reduce tension as students push in two different directions.

Completing the survey does not take much time, and reviewing the answers has been a game changer for the administrative team. They look forward to poring over the responses because they provide guidance for staff needs. Using the surveys helps ensure that resource allocations land in impactful places. Furthermore, a process typically considered an administrative task now includes teacher and staff input, creating a collective effort to plan school structures that work for everyone.

Scheduling

Just as scheduling can lessen frustration for adults, this same structural support can positively impact students. If students struggle to access the supports they need during the school day, they are unlikely to receive them at all (Mattos et al., 2025). Many scheduling-related tasks require strict adherence to rules, but looking for aspects open to your control and innovation can improve the daily experience for students and teachers.

Each summer, while the administrative team at Platinum High School examines the surveys, members also look at academic, attendance, and disciplinary data. The data points to higher percentages of discipline referrals for students receiving special education services. While this may be due to an issue with classroom management or instructional practices, this data uncovers a structural issue. When Jerry, the assistant principal, looks at the individual students and classes, he identifies a trend: The highest number of discipline referrals are for students who move from class to class together throughout the day. By the end of the day, some students receiving special education services have only been apart for one or two class periods.

First, Jerry takes the information to the principal and lead counselor. The lead counselor states that they have a few options to try and mix up the class schedules. She suggests two that would be the most feasible.

1. Look at the student rosters after the scheduling process runs and adjust accordingly.
2. Hand schedule selected students before running the scheduler.

After visiting with the special education department chair, Jerry determines that hand scheduling selected students will create the best learning environment possible for students and teachers. During the transition meetings from grade level to grade level, there is time to discuss the best learning environment. Adding a few minutes to the meeting and some extra summer work to the scheduling process could induce conflict if not everyone sees the value. However, the team, including the counselors, special education teachers, and assistant principals, sees how proactive work, mostly completed during the summer, will reduce issues throughout the year.

While examining the academic data, Zilia, the associate principal of instruction, notices students with drastic swings in achievement from class to class. For example, one student barely passed English, science, and social studies, but earned an honor-roll grade in mathematics. The data is not isolated to one or two students, and she cannot identify a particular subject or teacher with positive correlations. Then Zilia stumbles on what might be the answer: The students who had advisory time with a content teacher, even if it was not their teacher, tended to earn a higher grade in that subject. From that data point, Zilia began the process of researching whether her thought was correct.

After figuring out the advisor could influence course grades, Zilia set to work on ways to assign students effectively. She created a system that did not add too much additional work to others' plates for scheduling but would place students in groupings that provide more opportunities to make advisory time useful. In the first year, students were placed in their advisory groups based on data and demographics. Zilia balanced the classes considering the following student factors.

- Male and female
- Specific populations
- High need versus low need academically
- High need versus low need behaviorally
- High need versus low need attendance rate

The data Zilia already used in the summer to evaluate effectiveness guided the process to balance the classes. Balancing helped unify the staff because some teachers no longer had all high-need students and others all low-need students. It also helped camaraderie within the classes to balance the genders. Once again, all this data was already populated on the reports, so the structure simply took the information and made it useful.

After the first year, the team noted significant gains in achievement, lower discipline referrals during advisory time, and almost full staff buy-in for making the advisory system work. There were fewer teacher-to-teacher and teacher-to-student conflicts. For the second year, teachers asked for structures to have students move to different classrooms for targeted and timely support. The teachers saw value in intervening with students who did not pass the previous state assessment, but they saw greater growth with students when they could intervene before a test on current content. The team decided to try moving students based on data twice a week to start. They also combined the needs of students receiving special education services and scheduled their daily advising time according to content-based needs. The structure continues to evolve and adjust for student and teacher needs, thereby increasing the conditions to improve motivation and job satisfaction. The advisory structure sometimes involved extra work, but teachers and administrators found value in the proactive approach.

Leadership Teams

Leadership teams provide opportunities for shared leadership, also referred to as *distributive leadership*. Shared leadership has been recognized as an important facet of school reform and improvement as multiple layers of leaders work to solve problems and improve student learning outcomes (Javornik & Klemenčič Mirazchiyski, 2023; Nguyen & Hunter, 2018; Taylor et al., 2019). The structure of a leadership team can take many forms, depending on the organization's needs. As you examine your current structure or create a new one, focus on making space for a diverse set of voices to communicate celebrations and frustrations. Creating avenues for clarity and effective communication beyond sole reliance on administrators will reduce the likelihood that small tensions will go overlooked. Leadership teams provide a proactive structure for addressing problems productively.

If you do not feel comfortable surveying the entire staff, or if you feel you need consistent voices contributing to the conversation, use your leadership teams at the campus or district level to elevate collaboration and increase conflict-solving opportunities before problems become destructive. At Challenge Elementary, two leadership teams guide campus functions: the instructional leadership team and the operations team. These two leadership teams work independently on specific tasks but have some overlap for attacking structural issues that affect the learning environment. The consistency of meeting throughout the year gives ample opportunity to course correct or respond to specific needs in a timely manner. The structures help lessen conflict and diffuse information effectively throughout the organization.

The district also uses leadership teams for a similar purpose. The district has an instructional leadership team with several branches. At some points during the year, the entire team meets. At other points, the team divides up into principals, assistant principals, instructional coaches, and curriculum staff to tackle problems or disseminate information pertinent to each context. Having the district and campus structures in place provides opportunities for creating decision maps and producing a conflict-management plan that honors various stakeholders' needs and preferences. We dig into this structure more in chapter 7.

Training

Training structures tend to be limiting and cause frustration due to a lack of leveling and personalization. However, the professional development and training structures you put in place can also foster autonomy, competence, and relatedness (Dysvik & Kuvaas, 2014; Jansen in de Wal, van den Beemt, Martens, & den Brok, 2020). Whether at the district or campus level, training should fall into the following categories.

- **Appropriately leveled:** Will both new and veteran teachers or staff have opportunities for learning?
- **Personalized:** Will teachers or staff have a choice in pathways or presentations they attend?
- **Collaborative:** Will teachers or staff have an opportunity to work with peers and colleagues?

For now, consider how training structures contribute to the SDT conditions described in chapter 5. Chapter 7 will include more information about specific components and strategies related to the overall conflict-management plan.

Curriculum

Curriculum as a structural component shows up in resources. Some districts provide extensive resources and scripted curricula for teachers to use daily. Other districts provide basic overviews as a suggested guide for teaching standards. Both strategies provide structural pros and cons.

Extensive resources provide a step-by-step plan of action to teach standards and ensure student learning occurs. This can be a tremendous help for new teachers, but it significantly lowers autonomy. Additionally, making the use of district resources non-negotiable can provide consistency and alignment from campus to campus, better equipping district staff to effectively and efficiently assist with larger volumes of people.

The drawbacks emerge in the art of teaching and responsiveness to student need. Digging into standards, breaking down what needs to be taught, and determining how to teach it, how to assess learning, and how to support student needs become more difficult when one is not steeped in the process (DuFour et al., 2024; Power & Goodnough, 2019). When teachers are not active participants, they may struggle to sustain their *why* and struggle with the *how* when challenges arise that exceed what has been given to them. As a teacher, if I just show up and read what someone handed me, the lesson will lack authenticity and responsiveness, leading to student engagement issues (Dresser, 2012; Moussa, Louge, Pauwelyn, Contreras-Gomez, & Cao, 2024). If I have worked to create the lesson, a greater chance of ownership develops. Some schools lack the flexibility to use teacher-created resources, but even when a school uses scripted lessons, allowing for teacher-led adjustments along the way can increase teacher autonomy and student success (Moussa et al., 2024).

The lack of curriculum resources produces the opposite issues. If teachers are expected to create lessons, assessments, interventions, and extensions within a suggested guide or list of required standards, they will become more proficient at lesson design and at responding to students' needs, but there is no guarantee of consistency or fidelity from campus to campus or classroom to classroom. Data-driven instruction thrives through structures to consistently evaluate data with common markers. If we wait until the end-of-the-year assessments, adjustments and course corrections will be too late. The data may show outcomes were achieved, but there needs to be a check-in with teachers and staff about the sustainability of creating the resources and still having time to complete the other job requirements.

Responses to Systemic Issues

Campuses and districts operate within a vast system full of flaws. Why can't we all get along? Perhaps the real question is, "Why would we expect to get along when we are set up for failure before we get students inside the doors?" Honestly, these thoughts cross my mind at least twice a month and sometimes twice an hour of each day. I do not want to sugarcoat the systemic issues we face daily in education. There are too many standards to learn, standardized testing occurs without regard to a student's body of work, and the application of ever-changing state, provincial, and federal regulations can bring us down. However, the structures we put in place must focus on what we *can* control. We cannot control the number of standards we are expected to teach, the state assessment, or the laws added or changed each year, but we can put in place structures to ensure all students learn at a high level and teachers feel motivated and satisfied with their work.

One way to respond to systemic issues is adopting schoolwide and districtwide collaborative processes, such as the PLC at Work process. Such processes help schools implement structures that improve learning for all students. In the case of PLC at Work, every part of the process draws together all members of the organization to work collaboratively and addresses the systemic issues plaguing an education system. For further information on the PLC at Work process, start with the following resources.

- *Learning by Doing: A Handbook for Professional Learning Communities at Work* (4th ed., 2024) by Richard DuFour, Rebecca DuFour, Robert Eaker, Thomas W. Many, Mike Mattos, and Anthony Muhammad
- *Taking Action: A Handbook for RTI at Work*™ (2nd ed., 2025) by Mike Mattos, Austin Buffum, Janet Malone, Luis F. Cruz, Nicole Dimich, and Sarah Schuhl
- *The Big Book of Tools for Collaborative Teams in a PLC at Work* (2020) by William M. Ferriter

Scenarios for Reflection: Structures for Success

This chapter examined six different issues within various schools, focusing on structural needs to reduce conflicts. Use the two following scenarios to determine structural needs and improvements. As you work through the scenarios, think about how each element explored throughout the book connects to others.

Scenario 1

Throughout the year, the instructional leadership team (ILT) at Discovery Middle School worked on an updated mission and vision to present to the staff. Before the presentation, the ILT generated questions and planned responses to pushback on key factors. During the meeting, the staff bring up a few revisions to improve the mission statement. Most of the ILT welcomed the suggestions and felt encouraged to see how the staff bought into the process. The science department chair, however, who serves on the ILT, did not think the revisions significantly changed anything and did not see why this step was necessary. He thought the meeting could have been canceled or it could have been an email. On reflection after the meeting, the comments from the science department chair were the only ones that leaned toward negative.

Scenario 2

The fourth-grade team's data, both academic and discipline related, moved in a negative direction during the second quarter. The benchmark data dropped by 8 percent, and the discipline referrals increased by 9 percent. Assistant principals typically pop into meetings whenever possible, but the assistant principal starts attending the fourth-grade weekly team meetings consistently. She notices that the team leader speaks more than the rest of the team. She also notices that the team leader follows an agenda, but team members do not have access to the meeting agenda or notes. Finally, she notices that the curriculum resources do not provide thorough guidance. As a result, the teachers take what the team leader proposes and use that. They do not feel they can ask questions or make each lesson their own.

Figure 6.3 lists the topics of each chapter. For each scenario, determine what you would improve to lessen each type of conflict.

Conclusion and Next Steps

This chapter focused on the structures behind the scenes that directly affect conflict within organizations. After we broke down each structure, ideas and strategies for improvement helped you think through what each structure looks like in your own context. Applying what you have learned throughout the book and making connections lead us to the last chapter, where we will create a comprehensive conflict-management plan.

Strong structures help you approach conflict proactively instead of reactively addressing conflicts when people already feel tension. Use the reproducible "Proactive Planning" (page 147) to identify structural strengths and weaknesses. Use the "Chapter 6 Next Steps: Structures for Success" reproducible (page 150) to reflect on what you've learned about creating structures for success.

	Chapter 1	Chapter 2	Chapter 3:	Chapter 4	Chapter 5	Chapter 6
Chapter scenario 1	**Topic:** Clarify roles and responsibilities and improve communication. **Question to consider:** What needs to be clarified?	**Topic:** Categorize the conflict (curriculum, personality, or external pressures). **Question to consider:** What type of conflict is happening?	**Topic:** Choose an approach (absorb, tackle, or defer). **Question to consider:** What approach will most likely lead to a productive conflict?	**Topic:** Consider preferences and identity (task, relationships, overall), function, and hot buttons. **Question to consider:** How can you use personal preference and identity to improve the situation?	**Topic:** Maintain or improve conditions (autonomy, competence, and relatedness). **Questions to consider:** What actions need to take place? How do those actions affect the conditions?	**Topic:** Assess structural needs. **Question to consider:** What structural needs could be improved?

FIGURE 6.3: Chapter scenario reflection.

continued →

	Chapter 1	Chapter 2	Chapter 3:	Chapter 4	Chapter 5	Chapter 6
	Topic: Clarify roles and responsibilities and improve communication. **Question to consider:** What needs to be clarified?	**Topic:** Categorize the conflict (curriculum, personality, or external pressures). **Question to consider:** What type of conflict is happening?	**Topic:** Choose an approach (absorb, tackle, or defer). **Question to consider:** What approach will most likely lead to a productive conflict?	**Topic:** Consider preferences and identity (task, relationships, overall), function, and hot buttons. **Question to consider:** How can you use personal preference and identity to improve the situation?	**Topic:** Maintain or improve conditions (autonomy, competence, and relatedness). **Questions to consider:** What actions need to take place? How do those actions affect the conditions?	**Topic:** Assess structural needs. **Question to consider:** What structural needs could be improved?
Scenario 2						

Visit ***go.SolutionTree.com/leadership*** *for a free reproducible version of this figure.*

Proactive Planning

Use this reproducible to identify structural strength and weakness in your own school or district. As you complete the table, consider the three conditions of autonomy, competence, and relatedness. Then, answer the three questions that follow the table.

Area	Is this a structural strength or weakness or does it not apply to us?	If the area is a strength, what structures do we have in place? If the area is a weakness, what structures could we put in place to improve?	What is our next best step to sustain the category as a strength or improve a weakness? Who will monitor progress or lead the action plan?
Mission, vision, values, and goals			
Agendas			
Norms			
Meeting structures			

Area	Is this a structural strength or weakness or does it not apply to us?	If the area is a strength, what structures do we have in place? If the area is a weakness, what structures could we put in place to improve?	What is our next best step to sustain the category as a strength or improve a weakness? Who will monitor progress or lead the action plan?
Resource allocation			
Scheduling			
Leadership teams			
Training			
Curriculum			
Response to systemic issues			

1. What areas require the most structural improvements? Are there opportunities to decrease destructive conflict through the improvements?

2. How will you measure your return on investment? In other words, how will you determine whether the extra time spent on structural work sufficiently decreased conflict to make the work worth it?

3. How will you sustain or improve the conditions of autonomy, competence, and relatedness based on your action plans?

Chapter 6 Next Steps: Structures for Success

Individually or with team members or colleagues, use the following questions to reflect on what you've learned about structural configurations.

1. What's one structural strength we can identify? How do we know that it's a strength?

2. What's one structural weakness we can identify? How do we know that it's a weakness?

3. Which weakness do we most need to address? What would we include in an action plan to improve that weakness?

7

What Is the Plan?

CREATING A COMPREHENSIVE CONFLICT-MANAGEMENT PLAN

We have reached the point in the journey where you will combine the skills you've learned and the work you've done to create a comprehensive conflict-management plan for your district, campus, department, or team. This is a process, not a one-time event or reproducible document that never needs revision. In fact, your plan may not be contained in a single document. You will leave the chapter and book equipped with conflict-management skills to maintain and improve the SDT conditions in your organization. Pair the documents and action plans you create with response skills that help you analyze the moment and respond appropriately: That's the comprehensive conflict-management plan. This combination of instruments and tools keeps conflict productive.

You should create your conflict-management plan in sections over time and revisit it at least once a year. We work in a people business, and the variables when working with people create completely unique situations daily. Even when you have successfully implemented processes and plans, you will still need to maintain, sustain, and improve them over time and when people or situations change. These documents, structures, and plans belong to you; add what you need to proactively plan and keep conflicts productive. Also, recognize the importance of intangibles. Knowing which type of conflict is happening and which approach might best maintain a productive environment is paramount to implementing a successful plan. Those skills are difficult to quantify, but it is easy to recognize when they are not present through an increase in destructive conflicts.

This final chapter takes you through a year of implementation in Productive ISD, including the district and campuses involved in the work. Additionally, the chapter provides guidance for those at the campus or team level who want to increase productive conflict and decrease destructive conflict on a smaller scale. Finally, we will explore the importance of training and applications for various groups to sharpen the skills that will have the most influence on positive outcomes.

What to Do and When

The work of conflict management is no small task and must be ongoing. The following sections break down a schedule of manageable chunks for Productive ISD as it works to proactively approach conflict management through planning, professional development, and reflection.

Summer

Productive ISD's summer work on a conflict-management plan includes district and campus administrative contributions. While teachers and students take time to recharge and prepare themselves for another school year, the administrative teams proactively addresses some of the time-consuming work required to decrease role ambiguity and prepare for the current roster of staff and students. Whether at the district or campus level, here are the tasks to be completed.

- Support plans and decision mapping
- Communication flow
- Survey and data review
- Training and professional development opportunities

The following sections explain these tasks in detail.

Support Plans and Decision Mapping

During the summer, district- and campus-level administrators complete their portions of decision mapping to reduce role ambiguity and lessen frustration due to a lack of clarity. Most Productive ISD administrators return on contract during July. The superintendent and assistant superintendents first meet to discuss personnel changes at the administrative level. Noting strengths and weaknesses based on staff surveys, organizational health documentation, and state standardized testing data, the district administrative team highlights needs and creates an action plan for professional development and support at the campus level. Table 7.1 (page 154) shows a portion of the document the district administrative team created.

After completing the process for the campuses, the district administrative team also completes the process for the district staff and begin decision mapping. Evaluating campuses and planning action before decision mapping helps the district forecast possible needs and plan for possible sources of conflict. Notice the potential challenges at ABC Elementary in table 7.1, specifically in the staff survey and organizational health data column. Based on the data and surveys, a shift in student need currently does not affect the student data markers. However, the stress has started affecting the staff. They see how things are changing, and if they keep doing the same things that have typically worked in the past, the scores will probably start to plummet. Helping school leaders find reasons to continuously improve when the students usually score well may involve resistance. However, helping the administrative team see how to address staff concerns and tensions is a great start. Completing this exercise should not be time consuming, but it will give district leaders some perspective on possible needs instead of waiting until scores drop and teachers quit to address the conflicts.

At the July meeting with all administrators, the district presents the initial decision map and begins collaborating with campuses to create a more comprehensive document. During in-service and in the fall semester, the campus administrators will work with teacher leaders to continue the collaboration process. Table 7.2 (page 155) shows the rough draft of the decision map representing the large departments and focusing on how the departments work with the campuses. The administrative teams will use this as a starting point when working with their staff. The district staff finds the table format helpful for keeping the map clear and concise. Creating the initial maps might be chaotic, depending on the size of and layers within the organization, but getting past the initial difficulties can bring everyone into a clearer and more communicative space.

Communication Flow

While creating decision maps, district and campus leaders look for communication issues. Productive ISD district leaders noted that districtwide, students who receive special education services and English learners do not show growth at the same rate as their peers. Several conflicts that were substantial enough to make it onto their radar involved meeting the needs of those student populations. Additionally, they noticed that the special education and English learner

TABLE 7.1: Campus Evaluation and Action Planning

School	Personnel Changes	Staff Survey and Organizational Health Data	Staff Survey and Standardized Testing Data	Action Plan
Challenge Elementary	New assistant principal; was a teacher and team leader at Challenge Elementary, shadowed former assistant principal during internship	• High organizational health and survey data • Data shows administration consistently values staff input and encourages innovation to overcome challenges.	Standardized testing scores fall below state averages. However, year-to-year student growth measures are the highest in the district.	The administrative team continues to overcome obstacles and show growth in student learning. The group would benefit from help building community buy-in and implementing tiered instructional strategies.
ABC Elementary	New principal; was an assistant principal at Challenge Elementary	• Mixed results from organizational health and survey data • Data shows some staff feel there should be more work on student behavior. Some staff feel pressure to continue high-performance and achievement scores. Some note changes in student needs without a change in approach to instruction and behavior.	• High standardized test scores • Attendance rate has fallen 5 percent in the last year.	The new principal has a proven track record within the district. Support will be helpful in the transition from low parent involvement to high parent involvement. Principal will also need help with staff resistance to change.
Discovery Middle School	New assistant principal; has administrative experience	• High organizational health and survey data • Staff report feeling supported and valued. Staff also report that cycles of continuous learning help the administrative team and teachers work together to make changes that improve their experience and student learning.	• Consistent standardized test scores • Testing data positively reflected efforts to improve Tier 2 intervention and social studies systems.	This is the first time in almost a decade that Discovery will have a new member on the administrative team. The group might need support during the transition. The principal consistently works on improvements and stays up to date on current research and data trends. This means he normally pinpoints areas of refinement before swings in data show up at the district level.
Platinum High School	Same administration team	• Lower scores in staff morale this year • Data shows staff feel innovation can be difficult. Staff also report that student engagement has decreased in the last year.	• Standardized testing scores have remained consistent. • Growth measures have plateaued in several areas. Students receiving special education services and English learner scores are declining.	The administrative team would benefit from student engagement and data tracking support to help with growth measures.

TABLE 7.2: Rough Draft of District Decision Map

Area	Roles Involved	Responsibilities
Curriculum	Curriculum directors	• Set year at a glance, unit sequencing, and pacing for each subject • Create districtwide common assessments • Work with specialists to monitor and track student progress
	Curriculum specialists	• Work with grade-level teams to implement curriculum • Address strengths and weaknesses for all teams based on data
	Instructional coaches	• Work with grade-level teams, mainly at the campus level, to implement curriculum
Assessment	Assessment director	• Oversee all testing in the district • Train and monitor all campus testing coordinators
	Special education, English learners, and advanced academics directors	• Collaborate on dates and procedures for all standardized testing for their respective groups of students
	Campus testing coordinators	• Train staff on testing procedures • Plan and coordinate all testing
	Director of technology	• Coordinate technology needs with assessment staff at the district and campus levels
Special Education Services	Special education director	• Oversee all special education programming
	Special education assistant director	• Assist special education director in overseeing programs • Lead compliance training and oversight • Teach admission, review, and dismissal (ARD) preparation protocols
	Special education instructional specialists	• Guide implementation of specially designed instruction • Train teachers on best practices for ARD preparation
	Special education diagnosticians and ARD facilitators	• Work with directors and specialists to ensure compliance • Work with campus staff to schedule and conduct testing and ARD meetings

continued →

Area	Roles Involved	Responsibilities
504 Services	504 director	• Oversee 504 programs • Train campus 504 coordinator
	504 coordinators	• Conduct 504 meetings and complete necessary paperwork
English Learner Services	Director of bilingual education	• Oversee programs • Lead compliance training and oversight
	Campus LPAC administrators	• Ensure compliance • Work with test coordinator and lead teacher to conduct required testing
RTI Programs	English department	• Lead RTI work related to reading and writing
	Mathematics department	• Lead RTI work related to mathematics
	Special education department	• Develop protocols and procedures for student intervention teams moving from RTI to special education testing
	Campus academic deans and associate principals	• Lead campus RTI programs • Lead student intervention teams
Instructional Support	All curriculum directors	• Provide instructional support to all campuses
	Instructional technology specialists	• Help all campuses incorporate technology
	Instructional coaches	• Help all campuses with best practices and instructional support
Other	Human resources staff	• Facilitate proper hiring and employment procedures for all campus and district personnel
	Finance department	• Provide budget information for all departments and campuses • Implement spending protocols and procedures for all campus and district personnel

departments interact with teachers and staff minimally throughout the year in comparison to the curriculum staff. This reduces the amount of time available to build trust and contributes to some of the communication clogs in the system.

The curriculum department has already begun working with the other departments to improve learning outcomes for all students. Productive ISD has seen a substantial increase in students qualifying for special education services and English learners. Not only has the number of students increased, but the needs are also more varied and extreme. Since the curriculum department meets frequently with campus staff, they will begin incorporating short updates and information concerning student population departments throughout the year during meetings and in newsletters. This effort aligns with systems already in place, so it does not add extra work to anyone's plate. The goal is to simplify communication flow and make sure the different departments avoid isolation, confusing crossovers, and unnecessary conflicts.

The decision map sheds light on many of the crossovers between departments. To meet the needs of all staff, the district personnel made the following communication commitments.

- We will make every effort to respond to emails and phone calls within twenty-four to forty-eight hours.
- If the question is best answered by someone else, we will communicate with the person asking the question and the person best equipped to answer the question.
- If similar questions continuously come up, we will discuss the possible lack of clarity in roles, responsibilities, or training.
- When we feel we need support to ensure communication remains accurate, clear, consistent, and timely, we will ask for help.
- We will revisit our communication commitments once per semester or more often if needed.

Looking at the decision maps can be stressful. The examples included in this chapter and chapter 1 highlight how many opportunities for confusion and conflict exist within every decision. Planning for expectations and opportunities to fix problems or avoid potential issues can start with a simple commitment to effective communication.

Survey and Data Review

Remember, the goal of creating a comprehensive conflict-management plan is being proactive about increasing the probability of productive conflict. Without decision mapping and analyzing organizational data to improve communication flow, there would be a lagging response. Waiting and reacting means we respond to a steep decline in scores or a mass exodus of teachers and staff. Once those occur, we have already fallen victim to destructive conflicts. Examining data, searching for trends, and taking action to improve clarity and conditions can help the organization weather storms more effectively.

Productive ISD consistently completes organizational health surveys. Several campuses have started completing more specific and open-ended surveys as well. The data combination provides information to anticipate need. Productive ISD has committed to using the data to make small adjustments. They do not want to swing the pendulum too far in another direction and end up with unanticipated ripple effects that cause more harm than good.

Additionally, the district- and campus-based administrative teams have worked to evaluate the data without bias or prejudice. The teams work to put away preconceived notions and their egos to create the best learning environments for students and staff. This exercise helps the district and campus administrative staff value the human side of their jobs throughout the year. The delivery of constructive criticism can be conflict inducing. The summer process of evaluating data and surveys gives the team a chance to process how information delivery feels. Additionally, they can see how the SDT conditions of autonomy, competence, and relatedness play out in their own roles. They commit to practicing difficult conversations with each other to ensure their information delivery maintains or improves conditions.

Training and Professional Development Opportunities

Productive ISD offers summer training and professional development opportunities to all employees. This summer, the district offers pertinent training on key programs used in different departments to help with role clarity. They also offer opportunities to learn and grow in instructional strategies. The offerings are not required, but the district is finding that people show up and want to learn when the trainings have the following characteristics.

- Appropriately leveled
- Personalized
- Collaborative

Notice the connection to the SDT conditions described in chapter 5.

- ***Appropriately leveled* links to *competence*:** People want to feel they can digest the information and apply it with fidelity.
- ***Personalized* links to *autonomy*:** People want to feel they have a choice in how they use and apply the learning.
- ***Collaborative* links to *relatedness*:** People want to build relationships with other professionals who share the same wins and losses throughout the school year.

Making sure training includes the three factors linked to the SDT conditions has improved attendance. Additionally, the results from reflections and surveys at the end of the training courses have improved.

Some states or contracts might not allow for summer opportunities. In Productive ISD, staff attend by choice, and the summer work can be used for trade-out days throughout the year. Productive ISD's trade-out-day program provides teachers and staff the opportunity to attend professional development days in the summer or during the year, depending on teacher and staff choice. In the past, people attended the summer dates out of compliance to check a box and have more breaks throughout the year. The focus of summer training has changed slightly, but many of the offerings remain the same. However, reframing the training focus by linking lesson design to SDT conditions helps people feel more invested in the learning.

In-Service Time

Prior to school starting, most districts and campuses hold a week of in-service time to onboard new teachers, set initiatives for the year, and prepare for students entering the building. Think back to chapter 2 and the various types of conflicts school systems face (curriculum differences, personality differences, and external pressures). The in-service time crams all the conflict categories together into one week, but this time also tends to be a relative honeymoon period when most people are returning refreshed and ready for another year. The memories of the worst days from the previous year become romanticized into laughable stories from the trenches. Leaders must capitalize on in-service time when building and implementing a conflict-management system.

Throughout the summer, administrators plan and prepare for using this time to accomplish a list of tasks. It would be easy to overlook important conflict-management topics during this time, but skipping foundation work results in more destructive conflicts throughout the year. To be clear, the conflict work during in-service does not equate to icebreakers and team-building activities. Some people enjoy those activities, but others do not. Any activity should relate to a goal and specific outcome to ensure people know what will happen and why. Following are some items that you might accomplish during your in-service time.

- **Reinforce mission, vision, values, and goals:** Whether creating or updating, you can use in-service time to make sure everyone is headed in the same direction.
- **Create team norms:** The goal is to complete various activities that help groups learn about each other's strengths and weaknesses in a low-risk way before the situations become personal. High-quality team norms revisited and revised throughout the year can reduce potential conflicts and offset personally identified weaknesses.
- **Establish or reinforce procedures and protocols:** The in-service to-do list can feel disconnected from the work of student learning. However, reframing that work can lessen frustration and maintain productivity. Ask yourself these questions: "How can we bring clarity to the job role while learning procedures and protocols for everything from attendance to fire drills to required paperwork? Additionally, what do we need to present now versus once school starts?" More on the specifics of training is to come.
- **Highlight campus-specific initiatives:** As with procedures and protocols, there will be necessary presentations during in-service time to help staff understand expectations for the upcoming school year. When determining campus-specific initiatives, ask yourself these questions: "What were our strengths last year, and how will we build on those? What were our weaknesses last year, and how do we plan to improve?" Those are the questions and answers that will elicit buy-in. It's not a program or next new thing; it's another cycle of inquiry that improves the organization over time.

Although this list is not exhaustive, you can see how each Productive ISD campus will be able to address campus specifics with a common goal in mind. In-service time can be useful and help organizations achieve their goals. The time to increase role clarity, learn what colleagues have to offer, and plan for the potential pitfalls of the year yields positive results. These requirements then move out of the compliance zone and help staff to commit authentically. Commitment and purpose build trust. Think about chapter 4—combining task completion and relationships leads to teams that get the job done and enjoy the process of getting there together. Instead of thinking about in-service time as a boring slog, consider that each component should improve clarity and build relationships. This critical step in the process becomes an integral part of the conflict-management plan.

First Semester

A remnant of the honeymoon period remains in the first semester, giving staff a chance to settle in without becoming complacent or riddled with conflict. During this time, staff members have the opportunity to grow their knowledge of conflict categories and approaches.

As the early days of the semester pass, specific situations might pop up that provide chances to figure out whether the work completed during in-service time works in practice. Once again, the framing of this work during this time is paramount to successfully planning for and navigating conflicts. This time helps everyone refine what they thought might be best, with the data pointing to what adjustments need to be made. Because this work is part of having a sound conflict-management plan, the adjustments are made to documents and plans, not people.

For example, the student services department proposed setting communication response times to twenty-four hours, but in several situations, the staff had to contact the district lawyers for clarification on Title IX investigations. They made an adjustment to their plan, stating twenty-four hours unless contact with staff outside of the district is needed. That way, the campus-level administrators would know why some questions took longer than others to answer. An adjustment to the plan was made and communicated to the appropriate staff. No one in the student services department was reprimanded or excluded from the group because they could not meet the demands of the plan. Additionally, the parameters were not discarded or loosened to the point of frustration for those needing important communication. Remember that no one should feel out of control, incompetent, or removed from favor within the group, department, or campus. By focusing on what works or does not work about the plans, the adjustments should feel less intimidating.

As the semester progresses, the honeymoon will inevitably end, but specific groups will still have ample opportunities for timely and targeted professional development. At several campuses in Productive ISD, the administration and various teachers and staff present weekly professional development and training. Most offerings are voluntary, but some groups, including new teachers or teachers in need of assistance, attend specific trainings to improve capacity. Many opportunities reduce confusion, which reduces frustration. Figure 7.1 shows some of the offerings and reasoning for timing.

Platforms	People	Strategies
Learning management system • Builds on initial district training during new teacher in-service time Gradebook • Builds on initial training provided by the district • Always scheduled the Tuesday before the first round of grades are due Special education and English learner platforms • Builds on initial training provided by the district • Expands on campus-specific needs and covers basics after school has started and students are in the system Data platform • Builds on initial training provided by the district • Usually scheduled several times throughout the first semester and leveled for beginner, intermediate, and advanced users	Filling out special education, 504 plan, and MLL paperwork • Always scheduled the week before progress-monitoring paperwork is due Grade-level team time • Brings together different content teachers from the same grade level to collaborate and problem solve together Difficult conversations • Scheduled throughout the year • Can be targeted for different groups Who can help me? • Scheduled in first month of school • Focused on new teachers and teachers new to the campus or district	Intervention and extension • Scheduled throughout the school year and taught by various teacher leaders • Teacher leaders set the level and focus Data tracking and progress monitoring • Scheduled throughout the school year and taught by instructional coaches and administrators • Focus for each session is set based on time frame within the school year • *Example:* Using historical data to meet student needs from the start is held in September Classroom management • Scheduled throughout the school year and taught by assistant principals and teachers • Focus for each session is set based on time frame within the school year • *Example:* Training on strategies for consistent non-compliance is held in November Instructional design • Scheduled throughout the year and taught by various teachers and administrators

FIGURE 7.1: Campus Trainings

Think about how much information gets shared during in-service time and then look back at table 7.3. Some of the most common conflicts during the first semester develop because staff feel overwhelmed with information. How many new teachers have had an emotional outburst because they want to do a good job but simply don't know everything they need to about the hundreds of systems, tasks, and decisions required each day, and in some cases, each class period? Presenting the information in manageable chunks when it is needed has been a game changer for Productive ISD campuses. Administrators can see relief on the faces of new teachers who know what they need to do and how to do it. They can also see relief on the faces of veteran teachers who already know the ins and outs and aren't required to attend additional training sessions.

Keeping the trainings optional for most staff actually increased attendance and buy-in at Productive ISD. Veteran teachers who wanted to brush up on their knowledge felt free to attend, and several veteran teachers even volunteered to teach some of the sessions. All teachers also requested sessions to improve their craft and gain clarity. Although the initial goal was not to increase attendance or heighten teacher leadership potential, these unintended byproducts develop from the act of learning together. The staff builds community and trust as they learn together.

After attending a teacher's session on small groups, another teacher asked for additional strategies to make sure the rest of the class stayed on task. The teachers formed their own learning community and tracked improvements in student progress. If the same directive to improve classroom management during small groups came as a mandate from a supervisor, it could cause conflict. However, the outcome was positive for a multitude of reasons: The teacher made the choice to use small groups more effectively to improve student learning progress (autonomy), the teacher worked with another teacher instead of feeling incompetent with the supervisor (competence), and the teachers worked together on a common goal (relatedness).

Another group that meets consistently includes the team leaders and department chairs. A portion of those meetings is dedicated to conflict-management skills. The group members lead their peers and serve as intermediaries between teachers and administration. Simultaneously completing both will require additional work on leadership and conflict management specific to their leadership positions without supervisory authority. Learning how to categorize conflicts, approach each unique conflict, and improve the SDT conditions are issues the group will work on throughout the year together.

First-semester work focuses on refining what you thought might work best and preparing members of the organization for the rigors of their role. Revising maps and plans, updating norms based on needs, providing timely trainings, and even adjusting meeting times and locations can be worthwhile first-semester work. If you thought three o'clock in the afternoon on Tuesdays would work, but two team members serve on the curriculum adoption team that meets once a month on Tuesdays, change the meeting. If you have several new teachers that need additional training on the gradebook and grade expectations, add a training. If you have three sessions scheduled and everyone gets it during the first training, let the original participants know the following trainings are optional.

Second Semester

Building on the work done in the first half of the year, a comprehensive conflict-management plan should stay focused on continuous improvements and small tweaks where there are higher numbers of conflicts. The second semester tends to be when stress compounds and the small stuff starts to snowball. What might have been an easily managed conflict in the first semester can spiral into a destructive conflict during the second semester.

Phil, one of Productive ISD's assistant superintendents, notes the difference in managing conflicts since they began focusing on proactive plans and conflict-management training. As a former principal in the district, Phil remembers a team that started off with some low-level personality conflicts during the first semester. The team leader avoided the issue and decided they would just have to deal with a difficult personality. Once testing season and all the external pressures started to mount during the second semester, the team could not even meet without an administrator present. When Phil reflects on the situation, he can now see where a more proactive approach could have kept the conflict productive. He watched accomplished teachers fall apart and witnessed how the conflicts infiltrated the teachers' effectiveness in the classroom.

Eradicating the conflicts would not have perfected the teacher or student experience. Conflicts are inevitable, and addressing the conflicts could have improved the situation. However, the snowball rolled into an avalanche before anyone intervened. On reflection, Phil admits he was not prepared to handle the conflict. He sees the places where he would make different choices to lower the probability of destructive conflict.

Think back to your own experiences. What were those second-semester conflicts that spiraled into destructive conflicts? Consider whether there might have been a tension or frustration that lingered from the first semester. Sometimes a conflict spiral erupts out of nowhere, but other times you can isolate an event or a series of events leading up to the spiral. Don't overanalyze or regret but do reflect on ways to keep the conflict productive through summer and fall work.

End of School Year

By the end of the school year, most conflict management work centers on balancing the scales. Capturing where people are at before finishing out the year indicates unbalanced areas that you can focus on during summer work. It is important to remember that although we continuously attempt to balance the scales, conflict will always exist. Make sure to maintain perspective when analyzing survey data and reflecting on the year. Getting bogged down in the "what ifs" about decisions will not change what has already occurred. Use the information to guide the adjustments for the next year.

In Productive ISD, staff note how variables affect each other at every level. One team leader, Grace, notes that when feedback for topics related to tasks ranks high in survey data, there tends to be a drop in relationship data. She can also see how curriculum conflicts show up in score differentials. Finally, she sees how destructive conflict affects every area.

Through her work within her campus and throughout the district, Grace knows the first step is to focus on small adjustments that might improve the various areas. Last year, the team focused hard on data tracking to ensure all students were learning at a high level, but Grace can see how the team's hyper-focused attack on that task changed the team dynamic. Next year, she wants to make sure they continue with data tracking but include more teacher and student celebrations. That will be a team discussion and decision, but Grace wants to make it clear that the improvements in scores happened because of the people who put the systems in place. One teacher in particular struggled to maintain a positive outlook throughout the first semester. It caused some conflicts within the group, and Grace tried to absorb the venting and frustrations, as described in chapter 3. The conflict spiraled, but when Grace changed approaches and tackled the conflict, she identified the root cause and worked with the teacher and team to make adjustments. In hindsight, Grace feels strongly that she absorbed the conflict for too long. That does not mean she will immediately tackle every conflict next year, but she now knows what to look for in the team.

During the situation last year, relatedness and autonomy dropped. The team did not feel a sense of control or belonging during the worst parts of the conflict. Instead of banding together when they felt external pressures related to curriculum decisions, team members became hyper-focused on completing each task. That experience, combined with her reflection, will help Grace know better when to address issues and how. There is no time to overthink what she could have done differently, but she will use the experience to proactively adjust to lessen the probability of destructive conflict.

Conflict throughout the year is inevitable, but some years feel more peaceful than others. No matter what role you serve, collecting data for continuous improvement is a useful practice. If you end the year prepared to think about what next year looks like and how you want to improve, start that process right away. If you barely kept your head above the churning waves of conflict, let it rest. Collect the data and leave it. The data will keep, and you need to be in the right headspace to take action toward improvement. Give the data and conflicts time to breathe, but don't wait too long. When you dig into the data, assume positive intent. Every person who took the time to respond wants the organization to improve. Also, look for themes and trends. Take less time on the outliers and identify common insights, which will help you do more of what is working well and create action plans for improvement.

Large-Group, Small-Group, or Individual Approach

As you can see from the team leader's perspective relating to the end of the year in the preceding section, conflict-management plans and skills stretch to every corner of every building. Your district or campus may not be committed to creating a comprehensive plan, but individuals and small groups can make a difference. Whether you use this book to create an extensive plan for an entire district, learn skills and complete the work within a team, or simply work as an individual, you can affect the following changes, big or small, in your context.

- Improving clarity and communication lessens frustration (chapter 1).
- Categorizing common conflicts provides direction to specific areas of need (chapter 2).
- Choosing an approach allows for mindfulness regarding the most appropriate way to manage each unique conflict (chapter 3).

- Knowing ourselves and the people we work with helps prevent conflict spirals (chapter 4).
- Maintaining and improving SDT conditions can improve job satisfaction and motivation (chapter 5).
- Implementing structures for success proactively addresses potential conflicts (chapter 6).

No one wakes up each day wanting to feel miserable at work or feel like they are terrible at their job. If you or your colleagues are feeling miserable and you have made it to this final chapter, take action. Work internally on your responses to conflict or work with a small group to get clear on what you want to accomplish and how you plan to do that work. If student learning does not measure up to your expectations or the expectations of others, consider how conflicts might be getting in the way of student outcomes. However you feel as you read this section, take the next best step. Learning and growing your conflict-management skills will serve you well at work and in any context where you interact with people. Doing this work as a campus or district might move the mountains at a faster pace, but even a single person's improved response to a single conflict can move situations in a positive direction.

How to Develop a Training Plan

Creating a comprehensive conflict-management plan involves devoting a significant amount of time to prepping for conflicts. There is no way to anticipate every conflict and write a handbook or produce an if/then flowchart, but we can improve our conflict-management skills through training and development. I cannot emphasize enough that practicing these skills outside of the actual moment of conflict will yield better responses (Fisher, Ury, & Patton, 1991; Hocker et al. 2022). If we wait until the hot button activates and the heat of the moment explodes, the fallout can be destructive.

Training should be targeted, timely, and adjusted for need. To ensure that its training opportunities are productive and useful, Productive ISD uses the following questions.

- **Is the training appropriately leveled?** Will both new and veteran teachers or staff have opportunities for learning?

- **Is the training personalized?** Will teachers or staff have a choice in their pathways or the presentations they attend?
- **Is the training collaborative?** Will teachers or staff have an opportunity to work with peers and colleagues?

Several campuses in Productive ISD use scenarios during in-service time to get to know each other, learn conflict skills, and practice responses. This strategy improves results throughout the year as people own their shadow sides and recognize how the situations they practiced emerge within their own groups. Let's look at one campus and its trainings during in-service. This particular training involves the entire staff, and the content teams sit together in table groups. The campus instructional coach leads the activity and helps with questions.

> ***Campus instructional coach:*** *Now that we have covered some of the foundational skills of conflict management, let's dive into a scenario to practice our skills. To begin, each group will read the provided scenario, take one minute to think individually, and take two minutes to talk about what is happening in the situation before answering the three questions. I'll set the timer for ten minutes, and then we'll share some observations.*

The instructional coach provides everyone with the following scenario and the three questions that follow.

> *The seventh-grade team discusses intervention and extension for the upcoming unit at their weekly meeting. As Hermione tries to review the team norms and agenda, Ron tells jokes to Harry and Neville. Hermione begins to reprimand Ron and the team about how she must always do everything. Harry and Neville feel uncomfortable because they know how much work they need to do to prepare for the next unit. However, Hermione never lets them complete a task. To add to the stress of the moment, student performance on the essential standards in this upcoming unit has been some of the lowest for the last few years, and the eighth-grade team has explicitly asked for more attention to be placed on this unit.*
>
> 1. *What is happening in this scenario?*
> 2. *What conditions does each team member's choice affect?*
> 3. *How can the team keep this conflict productive?*

Table group one had the following conversation.

> ***Hanna:*** *This is a task-related conflict complicated by the friendships in the group.*
>
> ***David:*** *Clearly, Hermione likes being in control and cannot let anyone else do the work. She's probably jealous that everyone else in the group is friends.*

Hanna: *Ugh! The work must get done. It can't just be a party all the time.*

Sarah: *Guys, guys, you are both right, and it is also clear who leans into the task and who leans into the relationships within our table! Hermione's choices are making the group feel like they don't have a shot no matter what they do. If they feel like they don't measure up, why even try?*

Kelan: *Good point, Sarah, but I also think Hermione is feeling like an outsider in the group. So, what can they do to ease the tension and keep it productive?*

Kerry: *I bet Hermione can crank out a high-quality lesson in her sleep, but I bet Ron can make great connections with students. They need to use each other's strengths to improve student learning.*

Hanna: *Well, there you go! We didn't really address it, but for me, Harry and Neville are the most frustrating types from that scenario. At least Ron and Hermione are adding something to the group. Harry and Neville are just laughing along and then staying quiet.*

David: *I agree, Hanna. Be who you want to be, but don't just follow along with the crowd.*

As the instructional coach brings it back to the whole group, table groups finish up their conversations and make connections to common categories and approaches, what worked versus what needed improvement, and how they could consider people's preferences and the effects of their choices on the SDT conditions. After sharing, groups can see each other's perspectives and understand how everything they learned works together to reduce or increase conflict.

This leads into the next activity, where participants watch a thirty-second video clip of a team working together to solve a puzzle. After watching the clip, participants move to the left or right side of the room based on which team they would want to be on.

A couple of participants from each side of the room share why they would want that person on their team. One participant shares, "I am nothing like this person, but I would want them on my team to offset my weaknesses." Another participant agrees and adds, "I have never really thought about it, but some of the best years we have had were when the staff were different in personality and approach."

The instructional coach asks why that might be the case. The assistant principal adds that in her experience, it does not matter how similar or different the staff are when everyone is working toward the same goal. The instructional coach agrees, and as the staff move into the next portion of the training, they can see how everything fits together.

At a training session for the instructional leadership team consisting of team leaders and department chairs, the instructional coach and principal lead further scenario work with the teacher leaders. During this training, teacher leaders role-play responses to various conflicts and talk through strengths and weaknesses of the responses. Doing this work in a smaller group allows time to think through responses to common issues and increase possible responses and action plans. The work also provides a chance for teacher leaders to build relatedness as a group and help each other through common struggles.

From the variety of conflict management trainings offered throughout the year, the staff start to see how setting a common goal for each task clarifies where the group wants to go. No matter the group and no matter the work, the consistent focus on coming together is helping the campus achieve more with less tension. The campus has used this approach during work in the following areas.

- Mission, vision, values, and goals
- Essential standards
- Behavior strategies
- Curriculum implementation
- Student event planning
- Campus improvement plans

For each unique situation and each unique group working on the task, knowing where they want to go and how they are going to get there helps each person know what they can contribute to reaching the goal or completing the task.

These examples highlight a small sample of ideas helping Productive ISD campuses reduce destructive conflict and increase productive conflict. One of the most resistant assistant principals thought work on conflict management would be a waste of time. He said repeatedly, "We are all adults and professionals. We should be able to get along." After working through the process, he is already seeing how people can navigate situations without running to him for awkward interventions or interjections into random situations.

We are all adults and professionals, but we still need the tools and skills to handle the conflicts that arise in the difficult work of educating students. When we take the time to plan, prepare, and learn, we can do better for each other and our students. Our students deserve to operate in productive learning environments, and we do too!

Scenarios for Reflection: Creating a Comprehensive Conflict-Management Plan

These scenarios highlight opportunities to improve conflict management at different points in the year through different strategies learned throughout the book. As you read each scenario, think about how clarity, choices, considerations, conditions, and configurations could keep the conflict productive.

Scenario 1

During a required district professional development session in October, the curriculum leaders for the mathematics department review how to use a required system for practicing concepts and intervention. The program shows a strong correlation to standard mastery and standardized testing data, and the district purchased the program for every campus. As the group moves into a break, several teachers from several campuses approach the directors and specialists. The implementation has not gone well. The available technology does not consistently support the program. The teachers do not have rostered classes in the program, so they are spending hours trying to create classes, get students enrolled, and assign tasks to students. Although they see the value in the program, teachers are already starting to abandon it for more user-friendly resources. The user-friendly resources, however, do not directly connect to the standards or correlate with standardized testing success.

Scenario 2

In preparation for testing season, the general education and special education teachers sit down to plan out review stations for their classes. They create several group and individual activities based on benchmark data but come into a conflict over how to group the students on the last two days of the review. The general education teacher wants to group the students in need of special education services together so that the special education teacher can use specifically designed instruction to target student needs based on their disability and IEP. The special education teacher wants to continue grouping based on the specific learning target weaknesses exposed in the benchmark. They received different messages from the campus administration, mathematics curriculum staff, and special education department staff. They do not feel that any ideas are wrong or outside of best practice, but they also do not want to go against any campus or district directives.

For each scenario, answer the following questions.

1. In what part of the year is this scenario occurring?
2. At what time prior to the conflict emerging could the root causes have been addressed?
3. What needs to be addressed or understood to keep the conflict productive? Think about clarity (chapter 1), choices (chapters 2–3), considerations (chapter 4), conditions (chapter 5), and configurations (chapter 6).

Conclusion and Next Steps

In this chapter, we put together skills learned throughout the book and started the work of planning out when, where, and how to create a comprehensive conflict-management plan. The chapter began with manageable chunks to complete throughout the year for campuses and districts before applying to individuals and small groups. The chapter ended with training examples to guide the work of proactively planning and developing skills to increase productive conflict and decrease destructive conflict.

You have done the work! Now, create your conflict-management plan. Use the reproducible "Creating a Comprehensive Conflict-Management Plan" to identify the who, what, when, how, and why to complete the plan and then answer the questions that follow. Use the "Chapter 7 Next Steps: Creating a Comprehensive Conflict-Management Plan" reproducible (page 176) to reflect on what you've learned about plan creation.

Creating a Comprehensive Conflict-Management Plan

Area	Who does this area involve? Who is best equipped to lead this area?	What training or planning time will we need? What supports do we need to have in place for successful implementation?	When does work on this area need to happen? Is the work one time or throughout the year?	How will we implement our plan? How will we measure plan effectiveness in this area?	Why is this area important? How will our organization be better if we implement and carry out our plan?
Clarity: Decision mapping and communication work					
Choices: Understanding categories and approaches to make the best choices					
Considerations: Learning preferences, personalities, and hot buttons					

Area	Who does this area involve? Who is best equipped to lead this area?	What training or planning time will we need? What supports do we need to have in place for successful implementation?	When does work on this area need to happen? Is the work one time or throughout the year?	How will we implement our plan? How will we measure plan effectiveness in this area?	Why is this area important? How will our organization be better if we implement and carry out our plan?
Conditions: Understanding and improving autonomy, competence, and relatedness					
Configurations: Setting up the structures to improve the conditions					
Creation: Putting together the plan					

1. What area will be the easiest to complete? What area will be the most difficult? Why?

___

___

___

___

___

2. What would success look like if your plan works?

___

___

___

___

___

Chapter 7 Next Steps: Creating a Comprehensive Conflict-Management Plan

Individually or with team members or colleagues, use the following questions to reflect on what you've learned about plan creation.

1. How can we improve clarity and communication?

2. How might we teach and develop conflict-management skills?

    - How can we help staff categorize conflicts?

    - How can we help staff select a productive approach to managing conflicts?

3. How do people's personalities, tendencies, and hot buttons contribute to potential conflicts?

4. How can we best maintain or increase the SDT conditions of autonomy, competence, and relatedness?

5. Which structures and processes will most effectively manage conflicts we encounter throughout the year?

EPILOGUE

As the journey through Productive ISD and this book ends, the skills and strategies you've learned can help your teams, departments, campuses, and districts move toward productive conflict and away from destructive conflict. Use the various tools in each chapter to start conversations, proactively plan for inevitable conflicts, and build conflict-management skills within all areas of your organization.

Think back to all you have learned throughout the book to build a comprehensive conflict-management plan. The work should guide you through the following points.

- **Clarity:** By creating decision maps, our organization gained clarity about roles and responsibilities within the organization to reduce role ambiguity and improve communication.
    - Where: Chapter 1
    - How: Decision mapping
    - Why: A focus on clarity helps reduce role ambiguity and prepare for decision fatigue.
- **Choices:** After learning how to categorize common conflicts and determine an appropriate choice, our organization is better equipped to pinpoint specific areas of need and manage each unique conflict.
    - Where: Chapters 2 and 3
    - How: Categorizing common conflicts and selecting the best approach
    - Why: A focus on the appropriate conflict approach is rooted in understanding what the conflict stems from.
- **Considerations:** After completing various activities to learn about ourselves and our coworkers, our organization can more effectively avoid conflict spirals.
    - Where: Chapter 4

    - How: Evaluating task and relationship tendencies along with digging into personal hot buttons
    - Why: A focus on tendencies and personality traits helps us consider how each person's personal preferences can help or hinder the team.
- **Conditions:** After learning the educational applications of SDT, our organization can improve the conditions to increase job satisfaction and motivation.
    - Where: Chapter 5
    - How: Learning the SDT conditions and the importance of maintaining and sustaining autonomy, competence, and relatedness
    - Why: A focus on improving the conditions can heighten job satisfaction and motivation.
- **Configurations:** After exploring structural planning and implementation, our organization is prepared to proactively address potential conflicts.
    - Where: Chapter 6
    - How: Planning and implementing structures to increase clarity and improve the SDT conditions
    - Why: A focus on configuring structures to improve autonomy, competence, and relatedness helps us carry out our roles and responsibilities clearly.
- **Creation:** After reviewing key skills and concepts from the book, our organization can create a comprehensive conflict-management plan throughout the school year.
    - Where: Chapter 7
    - How: Using all the tools and skills throughout the book to create a comprehensive conflict-management plan
    - Why: A focus on creating a comprehensive plan provides extensive opportunity to talk about where the conflicts typically occur, plan to proactively address potential conflicts, and put structures in place to help staff thrive.

As you think through the journey, remember that conflict-management skills increase the likelihood of conflict being productive and lower the chances of destructive conflict. No two situations will ever be the same, and the same decision may not yield positive results every time. Since perfection remains unattainable, let us strive to help each member of the organization be better equipped to handle conflicts, manage conflicts, and recover from conflicts. When a conflict moves your organization forward, examine why your choices worked. Conversely, when a conflict does not turn out how you hoped, reflect on your choices and refine your skills. Either way, learn from each conflict and continue to improve.

Not only can you use the skills you've learned and the plans you've created throughout this book with members of your organization, you can also apply the same skills and plans to other situations.

- Between students and teachers or administrators
- Between parents and teachers or administrators
- Within IEP team or ARD committee meetings
- Within school board meetings

In each situation, think about the root of any conflict, your approach, who you are working with, the SDT conditions, and the structures. For example, many IEP team meetings involve conflict if the parents feel they do not have a voice in their child's education, or the meeting expectations are not clear. The same is true for interactions between students and teachers or administrators as well as parent meetings with campus or district staff. No matter who you are interacting with or what the exact context may be, the skills will be transferable.

Look to a future where you can quickly evaluate any situation and effectively manage a conflict. Not only will you be better equipped to keep the focus on student learning in your school system, you will also be better equipped to handle any interaction where conflict emerges. I thank you for taking action to grow your conflict-management skills because every person deserves to feel good about the job they do and the people around them.

REFERENCES AND RESOURCES

Alfauzan, A. A. H., & Tarchouna, N. (2017). The role of an aligned curriculum design in the achievement of learning outcomes. *Journal of Education and e-Learning Research*, *4*(3), 81–91.

American Psychological Association. (n.d.). *Conflict spiral. In APA Dictionary of Psychology*. Accessed at https://dictionary.apa.org/conflict-spiral on April 25, 2026.

Andersson, C., & Palm, T. (2018). Reasons for teachers' successful development of a formative assessment practice through professional development—A motivation perspective. *Assessment in Education: Principles, Policy & Practice*, *25*(6), 576–597. https://doi.org/10.1080/0969594X.2018.1430685

Ayoko, O. B., Härtel, C. E. J., & Callan, V. J. (2002). Resolving the puzzle of productive and destructive conflict in culturally heterogeneous workgroups: A communication accommodation theory approach. *International Journal of Conflict Management*, *13*(2), 165–195. https://doi.org/10.1108/eb022873

Ayub, N., AlQurashi, S. M., Al-Yafi, W. A., & Jehn, K. (2017). Personality traits and conflict management styles in predicting job performance and conflict. *International Journal of Conflict Management*, *28*(5), 671–694. https://doi.org/10.1108/IJCMA-12-2016-0105

Baumeister, R. F., & Vohs, K. D. (2007). Self-regulation, ego depletion, and motivation. *Social and Personality Psychology Compass*, *1*(1), 115–128.

Bisht, R., Uniyal, A. K., Johri, A., Qureshi, S. K., & Louati, H. (2025). Mapping the landscape of work-life balance of teachers: A bibliometric review of scholarly contributions. *Discover Sustainability*, *7*(1), Article 26. https://doi.org/10.1007/s43621-025-02222-5

Bouchart, F. J-C., Blackwood, D. J., & Jowitt, P. W. (2002). Decision mapping: Understanding decision making processes. *Civil Engineering and Environmental Systems*, *19*(3), 187–207.

Brodie, K. (2021). Teacher agency in professional learning communities. *Professional Development in Education, 47*(4), 560–573. https://doi.org/10.1080/19415257.2019.1689523

Brookhart, S. M., Guskey, T. R., Bowers, A. J., McMillan, J. H., Smith, J. K., Smith, L. F., et al. (2016). A century of grading research: Meaning and value in the most common educational measure. *Review of Educational Research, 86*(4), 803–848. https://doi.org/10.3102/0034654316672069

Carrell, S. E., Hoekstra, M., & Kuka, E. (2016). *The long-run effects of disruptive peers. American Economic Review, 108*(11). 3377–3415.

Chappell, S., Cooper, E., & Trippe, G. (2019). Shadow work for leadership development. *The Journal of Management Development, 38*(5), 326–335. https://doi.org/10.1108/JMD-08-2018-0216

Chiriac, E. H., Forsberg, C., & Thornberg, R. (2024). Teacher teams: A safe place to work on creating and maintaining a positive school climate. *School Psychology of Education, 27*(4), 1775–1795. Accessed at https://link.springer.com/article/10.1007/s11218-023-09880-1 on February 19, 2026.

Cohen, S. (Ed.). (2015). *APA dictionary of psychology*. American Psychological Association. Cohen, S. (2015). Article or entry title. In G. R. VanderBos (Ed.), *APA dictionary of psychology*. American Psychological Association.

Comes, T., Hiete, M., Wijngaards, N., & Schultmann, F. (2011). Decision maps: A framework for multi-criteria decision support under severe uncertainty. *Decision Support Systems, 52*(1), 108–118.

Conflict. (n.d.). In *Merriam-Webster's online dictionary*. Accessed at www.merriam-webster.com/dictionary/conflict on September 15, 2025.

Creagh, S., Thompson, G., Mockler, N., Stacey, M., & Hogan, A. (2025). Workload, work intensification and time poverty for teachers and school leaders: A systematic research synthesis. *Educational Review, 77*(2), 661–680. https://doi.org/10.1080/00131911.2023.2196607

Cummings, M. I., & Olson, J. D. (2020). The importance and potential of community partnerships in urban schools in an era of high-stakes accountability. *Improving Schools, 23*(2), 109–124. https://doi.org/10.1177/1365480219880129

Deci, E. L., & Ryan, R. M. (1985). *Intrinsic motivation and self-determination in human behavior*. Plenum.

De Clercq, D., Rahman, Z. M., & Belausteguigoitia, I. (2017). Task conflict and employee creativity: The critical roles of learning orientation and goal congruence. *Human Resource Management, 56*(1), 93–109. https://doi.org/10.1002/hrm.21761

Diehl, D. K., & Golann, J. W. (2023). An integrated framework for studying how schools respond to external pressures. *Educational Researcher, 52*(5), 296–305. https://doi.org/10.3102/0013189X231159599

Dresser, R. (2012). The impact of scripted literacy instruction on teachers and students. *Issues in Teacher Education, 21*(1), 71.

DuFour, R., DuFour, R., Eaker, R. E., Many, T. W., Mattos, M. W., & Muhammad, A. (2024). *Learning By Doing: A handbook for Professional Learning Communities at Work* (4th ed.). Solution Tree Press.

DuFour, R., DuFour, R., Eaker, R., Mattos, M., & Muhammad, A. (2021). *Revisiting Professional Learning Communities at Work: Proven insights for sustained, substantive school improvement* (2nd ed.). Solution Tree Press.

Dunn, A. (2023). *Professional learning community conflicts and teacher leader conflict management from multiple stakeholder perspectives* (Publication No. 565) [Doctoral dissertation, Abilene Christian University]. Digital Commons @ ACU. https://digitalcommons.acu.edu/etd/565

Dysvik, A., & Kuvaas, B. (2014). Self-determination theory and workplace training and development. In M. Gagné (Ed.), *The Oxford handbook of work engagement, motivation, and self-determination theory* (pp. 218–228). Oxford University Press.

English Standard Version Bible. (2001). Crossway Bibles.

Ferriter, W. M. (2020). *The big book of tools for collaborative teams in a PLC at Work.* Solution Tree Press.

Fisher, R., Ury, W., & Patton, B. (1991). *Getting to yes: Negotiating agreement without giving in* (2nd ed.). Penguin.

Franklin, B. (1772, September 19). [Letter to Joseph Priestley]. National Archive. Accessed at https://founders.archives.gov/documents/Franklin/01-19-02-0200 on February 17, 2026.

Frazier, M. L., Fainshmidt, S., Klinger, R. L., Pezeshkan, A., & Vracheva, V. (2017). Psychological safety: A meta-analytic review and extension. *Personnel Psychology, 70*(1), 113–165. https://doi.org/10.1111/peps.12183

Gallois, C., Watson, B. M., & Giles, H. (2018). Intergroup communication: Identities and effective interactions. *Journal of Communication, 68*(2), 309–317.

Gkiontsi, D., & Karanika-Murray, M. (2016). Dealing with economic and demographic challenges: Workplace innovation practices as a timely and effective response to older workers' needs. *European Journal of Workplace Innovation, 2*(1), 25–42.

Guskey, T. R. (2024). Addressing inconsistencies in grading practices. *Phi Delta Kappan, 105*(8), 52–57. https://doi.org/10.1177/00317217241251883

Hattie, J. (2016, July 11). *Mindframes and maximizers* [Conference presentation].Third Visible Learning annual conference, Washington, DC, United States.

Hattie, J. (2023). *Visible learning: The sequel—A synthesDCf over 2,100 meta-analyses relating to achievement.* Routledge.

Hobson, A. J., & Maxwell, B. (2017). Supporting and inhibiting the well-being of early career secondary school teachers: Extending self-determination theory. *British Educational Research Journal, 43*(1), 168–191. https://doi.org/10.1002/berj.3261

Hocker, J. L., Berry, K., & Wilmot, W. W. (2022). *Interpersonal conflict* (11th ed.). McGraw Hill.

Horton, K. E., Bayerl, P. S., & Jacobs, G. (2014). Identity conflicts at work: An integrative framework. *Journal of Organizational Behavior, 35*(S1), S6–S22.

Jansen in de Wal, J., van den Beemt, A., Martens, R. L., & den Brok, P. J. (2020). The relationship between job demands, job resources and teachers' professional learning: Is it explained by self-determination theory? *Studies in Continuing Education, 42*(1), 17–39. https://doi.org/10.1080/0158037x.2018.1520697

Javornik, Š., & Klemenčič Mirazchiyski, E. (2023). Factors contributing to school effectiveness: A systematic literature review. *European Journal of Investigation in Health, Psychology and Education, 13*(10), 2095–2111. https://doi.org/10.3390/ejihpe13100148

Jin, S., Singh, S., & Chaerin, Y. (2019). Reciprocally causal: The link between task and relationship conflict in teams. *Review of General Management, 30*(2), 68–96. Accessed at www.managementgeneral.ro/pdf/2-2019-5.pdf on October 7, 2025.

Johnson, P. R., & Indvik, J. (2001). Slings and arrows of rudeness: Incivility in the workplace. *Journal of Management Development, 20*(8), 705–714. https://doi.org/10.1108/EUM0000000005829

Jones, C. M., & Thessin, R. A. (2015). A review of the literature related to the change process schools undergo to sustain PLCs. *Planning & Changing, 46*(1/2), 193–211. Accessed at https://search.proquest.com/openview/07fe213482c54feb7e7fd81b2fae9bdb/1.pdf?pq-origsite=gscholar&cbl=47169 on March 2, 2026.

Kanat-Maymon, Y., Elimelech, M., & Roth, G. (2020). Work motivations as antecedents and outcomes of leadership: Integrating self-determination theory and the full range leadership theory. *European Management Journal, 38*(4), 555–564. https://doi.org/10.1016/j.emj.2020.01.003

Klein, E. J., Taylor, M., Munakata, M., Trabona, K., Rahman, Z., & McManus, J. (2018). Navigating teacher leaders' complex relationships using a distributed leadership framework. *Teacher Education Quarterly, 45*(2), 89–112. Accessed at https://files.eric.ed.gov/fulltext/EJ1175531.pdf on October 7, 2025.

Kolleck, N., Schuster, J., Hartmann, U., & Gräsel, C. (2021). Teachers' professional collaboration and trust relationships: An inferential social network analysis of teacher teams. *Research in Education, 111*(1), 89–107. https://doi.org/10.1177/00345237211031585

Kraft, M. A., & Monti-Nussbaum, M. (2021). The big problem with little interruptions to classroom learning. *AERA Open, 7*. https:doi.org/10.1177/23328584211028856

LeBlanc, L. A., & Nosik, M. R. (2019). Planning and leading effective meetings. *Behavior Analysis in Practice, 12*(3), 696–708. https://doi.org/10.1007/s40617-019-00330-z

Lee, A. N., Nie, Y., & Bai, B. (2020). Perceived principal's learning support and its relationships with psychological needs satisfaction, organisational commitment and change-oriented work behaviour: A Self-Determination Theory's perspective. *Teaching and Teacher Education, 93*, Article 103076. https://doi.org/10.1016/j.tate.2020.103076

Martinek, D. (2019). The consequences of job-related pressure for self-determined teaching. *Social Psychology of Education, 22*(1), 133–148. https://doi.org/10.1007/s11218-018-9446-x

Mattos, M., Buffum, A., Malone, J., Cruz, L. F., Dimich, N., & Schuhl, S. (2025). *Taking action: A handbook for RTI at Work* (2nd ed.). Solution Tree Press.

Mauersberger, H., Hess, U., & Hoppe, A. (2020). Measuring task conflicts as they occur: A real-time assessment of task conflicts and their immediate affective, cognitive and social consequences. *Journal of Business and Psychology, 35*(6), 813–830. https://doi.org/10.1007/s10869-019-09640-z

Moussa, W., Louge, N., Pauwelyn, L., Contreras-Gomez, R., & Cao, Y. (2024). Should teachers stick to the script? Examining the effects of scripted lessons on student literacy in Madagascar. *International Journal of Educational Research, 124*, Article 102290. https://doi.org./10.1016.j.ijer.2023.102290

Navo, M., & Williams, A. (2023). *Demystifying MTSS: A school and district framework for meeting students' academic and social-emotional needs.* Solution Tree Press.

Nguyen, T. D., & Hunter, S. (2018). Towards an understanding of dynamics among teachers, teacher leaders, and administrators in a teacher-led school reform. *Journal of Educational Change, 19*(4), 539–565.

Power, K., & Goodnough, K. (2019). Fostering teachers' autonomous motivation during professional learning: A Self-Determination Theory perspective. *Teaching Education, 30*(3), 278–298. https://doi.org/10.1080/10476210.2018.1465035

Pringle, T. A., & Robinson, M. D. (2024). The diversity advantage: An explanatory framework for personality traits. *European Journal of Personality, 38*(6), 867–888. https://doi.org/10.1177/08902070241228327

Printy, S. M., & Marks, H. M. (2006). Shared leadership for teacher and student learning. *Theory Into Practice*, *45*(2), 125–132. https://doi.org/10.1207/s15430421tip4502_4

Pruitt, D. G. (2001). Conflict and conflict resolution, social psychology of. In N. J. Smelser & P. B. Baltes (Eds.), *International encyclopedia of the social and behavioral sciences* (pp. 2531–2534). https://doi.org/10.1016/b0-08-043076-7/01797-6

Rahim, M. A. (2023). *Managing conflict in organizations* (5th ed.). Routledge.

Rasool, S. F., Wang, M., Tang, M., Saeed, A., & Iqbal, J. (2021). How toxic workplace environment effects the employee engagement: The mediating role of organizational support and employee wellbeing. *International Journal of Environment Research and Public Health*, *18*(5), 2294. https://doi.org/10.3390/ijerph18052294

Ryan, R. M., & Deci, E. L. (2000). Self-Determination Theory and the facilitation of intrinsic motivation, social development, and well-being. *American Psychologist*, *55*(1), 68–78. https://doi.org/10.1037/0003-066X.55.1.68

Ryan, R. M., & Deci, E. L. (2002). Overview of Self-Determination Theory: An organismic-dialectical perspective. In E. L. Deci & R. M. Ryan (Eds.), *Handbook of self-determination research* (pp. 3–33). University of Rochester Press.

Ryan, R. M., & Deci, E. L. (2017). *Self-Determination Theory: Basic psychological needs in motivation, development, and wellness*. Guilford.

Ryan, R. M., Deci, E. L., Vansteenkiste, M., & Soenens, B. (2021). Building a science of motivated persons: Self-Determination Theory's empirical approach to human experience and the regulation of behavior. *Motivation Science*, *7*(2), 97–110. https://doi.org/10.1037/mot0000194

Sheldon, S. B. (2007). Improving student attendance with school, family, and community partnerships. *The Journal of Educational Research*, *100*(5), 267–275. https://doi.org/10.3200/JOER.100.5.267-275

Shim, S. S, Finch, W. H., Cho, Y., Knapke, M. (2022). Understanding teachers' job satisfaction and flow: The dual process of psychological needs. *Educational Psychology*, *42*(3), 316–333. https://doi.org/10.1080/01443410.2021.1985970

Siburian, J., Corebima, A. D., Ibrohim, & Saptasari, M. (2019). The correlation between critical and creative thinking skills on cognitive learning results. *Eurasian Journal of Educational Research*, *19*(81), 1–16. https://doi.org/10.14689/ejer.2019.81.6

Stoll, L., Bolam, R., McMahon, A., Wallace, M., & Thomas, S. (2006). Professional learning communities: A review of the literature. *Journal of Educational Change*, *7*(4), 221–258. https://doi.org/10.1007/s10833-006-0001-8

Szulawski, M., Kaźmierczak, I., & Prusik, M. (2021). Is self-determination good for your effectiveness? A study of factors which influence performance within self-determination theory. *PLOS ONE, 16*(9), Article e0256558. https://doi.org/10.1371/journal.pone.0256558

Taggar, S., & Ellis, R. (2007). The role of leaders in shaping formal team norms. *The Leadership Quarterly, 18*(2), 105–120. https://doi.org/10.1016/j.leaqua.2007.01.002

Taylor, M., Klein, E. J., Munakata, M., Trabona, K., Rahman, Z., & McManus, J. (2019). Professional development for teacher leaders: Using activity theory to understand the complexities of sustainable change. *International Journal of Leadership in Education, 22*(6), 685–705. https://doi.org/10.1080/13603124.2018.1492023

van Bunderen, L., Greer, L. L., & van Knippenberg, D. (2018). When interteam conflict spirals into intrateam power struggles: The pivotal role of team power structures. *Academy of Management Journal, 61*(3), 1100–1130. https://doi.org/10.5465/amj.2016.0182

van Greunen, C., Venter, E., & Sharp, G. (2021). The influence of relationship and task conflict on the knowledge-sharing intention in knowledge-intensive organisations. *South African Journal of Business Management, 52*(1), Article a2166. https://doi.org/10.4102/sajbm.v52i1.2166

Wiliam, D. (2018). *Embedded formative assessment* (2nd ed.). Solution Tree Press.

Youn, M., (2018). The influence of standardized testing pressure on teachers' working environment. *KEDI Journal of Educational Policy, 15*(2), 3–22. https://doi.org/10.22804/kjep.2018.15.2.001

Ziegert, J. C., & Dust, S. B. (2021). Integrating formal and shared leadership: The moderating influence of role ambiguity on innovation. *Journal of Business and Psychology, 36*(6), 969–984. https://doi.org/10.1007/s10869-020-09722-3

INDEX

A

absorbing the conflict. *See also* common approaches to conflict
- about, 62
- deciding when absorbing is the right move, 64–66
- negative uses of, 63–64
- positive uses of, 62–63

academics and curriculum differences, 36–38
agendas, 131–134
autonomy, 109, 110–112
avoiding conflict spirals. *See* conflict spirals

B

behavior, 38–40
Berry, K., 1
bias, 94

C

clarifying roles and responsibilities in your organization. *See* roles and responsibilities within your organizations
clarity, need for, 8–10
common approaches to conflict
- about, 61–62
- absorbing the conflict, 62–66
- conclusion and next steps, 76
- deferring the conflict, 70–73
- obstacles that contribute to choice, 74–75
- questions for improving your conflict approach, 74
- reproducibles for, 78–81
- scenarios for reflection, 75–76, 77
- tackling the conflict, 66–70

common conflict categories in schools
- about, 35–36
- conclusion and next steps, 54
- curriculum differences, 36–45
- external pressures, 49–53
- personality differences, 45–49
- reproducibles for, 56–59
- scenarios for reflection, 53–54, 55

communication
- and effects of conflict on the organization, 89
- in the first semester, 161
- flow of, 23–25, 153, 157
- and leadership teams, 140

community partnerships, 51–52
competence, 109
compliance
- absorbing the conflict and, 62, 64, 65
- autonomy and, 110, 111, 112
- decision mapping and, 17
- norms and, 134

conflict
- approaches to. *See* common approaches to conflict
- categories of. *See* common conflict categories in schools
- definition of, 1
- managing. *See* creating a comprehensive conflict-management plan

conflict spirals
- about, 83–84
- conclusion and next steps, 98, 100
- effects of conflict on relationships, 87–88
- effects of conflict on task completion, 84–87
- effects of conflict on the organization, 88–91

go-to orientations and tendencies, 91–93
hot-button issues, 94–96
reproducibles for, 101–106
scenarios for reflection, 96–98, 99
Creagh, S., 26
creating a comprehensive conflict-management plan
about, 151–152
campus evaluation and action planning, 154
conclusion and next steps, 172
developing a training plan, 167–170
large-group, small-group, or individual approach, 166–167
reproducibles for, 173–176
scenarios for reflection, 171–172
what to do when, 152–166
curriculum differences. *See also* common conflict categories in schools
about, 36
academics and, 36–38
behavior and, 38–40
extensions and, 43–44
grading and, 41–42
instruction design and, 40–41
interventions and, 42–43
small stuff and, 44–45
curriculum structures for success, 141–142

D

decisions and decision mapping
about, 7, 10-11
communication and, 23-24
decision fatigue and, 25–27
examples for, 17, 18, 20, 21–22
roles and, 16–19, 23
rough draft for, 155–156
support plans and, 152–153
deferring the conflict. *See also* common approaches to conflict
about, 70–71
deciding when deferring is the right move, 73
negative uses of, 72–73
positive uses of, 71–72
distributed leadership, 140
district leadership, 14, 15. *See also* roles and responsibilities within your organizations

E

end of school year, 165–166
extensions, 43–44
external pressures. *See also* common conflict categories in schools
about, 49–50
community partnerships and parents and, 51–52
legislation and standardized testing, 50–51
social media and, 52–53

F

first semester, 161–164

G

gossip
absorbing the conflict and, 62, 65, 66
deferring the conflict and, 72, 73
effects of conflict on the organization, 91
tackling the conflict and, 70
grading, 41–42

H

Hocker, J., 1
how are we responding? common approaches to conflicts. *See* common approaches to conflicts
how can we keep conflict productive? improving job satisfaction and motivation. *See* improving job satisfaction and motivation

I

identity, 94, 96
implementing structures for success. *See* structures for success
improving job satisfaction and motivation
about, 107–108
conclusion and next steps, 123
reproducibles for, 124–126
scenarios for reflection, 120–122
self-determination theory and,

108–118
ways to improve the three SDT conditions, 118–120
initiatives and in-service time, 160
in-service time, 159–161
instruction design, 40–41
interventions, 42–43
introduction
goal of this book, 4–5
how it all began, 2–3
who should read this book, 3

L

leadership. *See also* roles and responsibilities within your organizations
distributed leadership, 140
district leadership, 14, 15
leadership teams, 140
legislation, 50–51
level of functioning, 116

M

meeting structures, 135
mission, vision, values, and goals
in-service time and, 160
structures for success, 130–131

N

norms
in-service time and, 160
structures for success, 134–135

O

organization charts
decision mapping and, 12
example organization chart, 11
example web structure for organization chart, 13

P

parents and external pressures, 51–52
personality differences. *See also* common conflict categories in schools
about, 45
personality traits, 45–48
work-life balance, 48–49

R

relatedness, 109, 116–118
relationships
effects of conflict on relationships, 87–88
relationship-orientation indicators, 93
reproducibles for
chapter 1 next steps: clarity, 33–34
chapter 2 next steps: categorizing, 58–59
chapter 3 next steps: approaching conflict, 80–81
chapter 4 next steps: avoiding conflict spirals, 105–106
chapter 5 next steps: improving conditions and motivation, 127–128
chapter 6 next steps: structures for success, 150
chapter 7 next steps: creating a comprehensive conflict-management plan, 176
creating a comprehensive conflict-management plan, 173–175
how are we responding? common approaches to common conflicts, 78–79
how can we keep conflict productive? creating conditions to improve job satisfaction and motivation, 124–126
layers of leadership, 30–32
proactive planning, 147–150
task or relationship orientation?, 101–102
what is happening? common conflicts, 56–57
who are we? using personal orientation to avoid conflict spirals, 103–104
resource allocation, 135–137
responses, 119–120
responsibilities, 115
roles and responsibilities within your organizations
about, 7–8
competence and, 113
conclusion and next steps, 29

decision mapping and, 10–27
example organization chart, 11
need for clarity, 8–10
reproducibles for, 30–34
scenarios for reflection, 28–29

S

scheduling, 138–140
second semester, 164–165
self-determination theory (SDT)
about, 108–109
autonomy and, 110–112
competence and, 112–116
relatedness and, 116–118
ways to improve the three SDT conditions, 118–120
shadow side, 46–48
social media, 52–53
standardized testing, 50–51
structures for success
about, 129–130
agendas, 131–134
conclusion and next steps, 144
curriculum, 141–142
leadership teams, 140
meeting structures, 135
mission, vision, values, and goals, 130–131
norms, 134–135
reproducibles for, 147–150
resource allocation, 135–137
responses to systemic issues, 142–143
scenarios for reflection, 143–144, 145–146
scheduling, 138–140
training, 141
ways to improve the three SDT conditions, 118–119
style, 87
summer
communication flow and, 153, 157
support plans and decision mapping and, 152–153
survey and data review and, 158
training and professional development opportunities, 158–159

T

tackling the conflict. *See also* common approaches to conflict
about, 66
how to decide when tackling is the right move, 69–70
negative uses of, 68–69
positive uses of, 66–68
task completion, effects of conflict on, 84–87
task orientation, 91–93
tasks, shifting from task to task, 115
tasks with higher difficulty, 113–114
toxic workplaces, 64
training
example for campus training, 162
how to develop a training plan, 167–170
structures for success, 141
training and professional development opportunities, 158–159
trust
conflict and, 66, 69, 70, 88
relatedness and, 117–118

W

what are the effects? avoiding conflict spirals. *See* conflict spirals
what can we be proactive about? implementing structures for success. *See* structures for success
what is happening? common conflict categories in schools. *See* common conflict categories in schools
what is the plan? creating a comprehensive conflict-management plan. *See* creating a comprehensive conflict-management plan
whose job is it? clarifying roles and responsibilities in your organization. *See* roles and responsibilities within your organizations
Wilmot, W., 1
work intensification, 26
work-life balance, 48–49

Giving It Your All Without Giving It All
Blake Clark
This is the guide to the human side of leadership. Blake Clark offers a workbook approach to self-preservation and sustainability that will help every principal define their leadership identity and lead with authenticity. Gain practical strategies to conserve energy and make complex decisions with courage.
BKG304

Together We Lead
Michelle Marrillia, Brittany Mozingo, and Rebecca Nicolas
The principal-coach partnership is one of the school's most powerful leadership teams. The authors provide a proven, four-phase framework for building professional trust and aligning on goals. Learn how to build true collaboration for lasting student impact.
BKG286

Facilitating Shared Success
Deb Page, Judith Hale, Jean Quigg, and Kayla Duncan
With tools, protocols, and real-world examples, this book empowers educators to lead with clarity, engage teams, and drive sustainable school improvement. Focused on improving human performance using the Certified School Improvement Specialist standards, it offers a systematic approach to collaborative inquiry and capacity building.
BKG273

Responding to Resistance
William A. Sommers
Educational leadership is never conflict free. In *Responding to Resistance*, author William A. Sommers acknowledges this reality and presents school leaders with wide-ranging strategies to decisively address conflict involving staff, students, parents, and other key stakeholders.
BKF955

Solution Tree | Press a division of Solution Tree

Visit SolutionTree.com or call 800.733.6786 to order.